Marketing Management and Strategy

Marketing Engineering Applications

Gary L. Lilien
The Pennsylvania State University
Arvind Rangaswamy
The Pennsylvania State University

Second Edition

Co-sponsored by

Institute for the Study of Business Markets

Prentice Hall
Upper Saddle River,
New Jersey 07458

Acquisitions editor: Bruce Kaplan
Associate Editor: Melissa Pellerano
Assistant editor: Danielle Rose Serra
Media Project Manager: Anthony Palmiotto
Production editor: Carol Zaino
Manufacturer: Integrated Book Technology

Copyright ©2003 by Prentice-Hall, Inc., Upper Saddle River, New Jersey, 07458. All rights reserved. Printed in the United States of America. This publication is protected by copyright, and permission should be obtained from the publisher prior to any prohibited reproduction, storage in a retrieval system, or transmission in any form or by any means, electronic, mechanical, photocopying, recording, or likewise. For information regarding permission(s), write to: Rights and Permissions Department.

ISBN 0-13-008463-8
10 9 8 7 6 5 4 3 2

Contents

Preface v

Conglomerate's New PDA Case 1

ABB Electric Segmentation Case 11

Product Planning Using the GE/McKinsey Approach at Addison Wesley Longman Case 15

Positioning the Infiniti G20 Case 23

Syntex Laboratories (A) Case 31

ADCAD Ad Copy Design Exercise 55

To my love and best friend,
Dorothy, for sharing her time
with one more book
—Gary

To Ann for her love and support,
and Cara for providing the
needed distraction.
—Arvind

Preface

Rapid changes in the marketplace, in data availability, and in the computing environment are transforming the structure and content of the marketing manager's job. As a profession, marketing is evolving so that it is no longer based primarily on conceptual content and, increasingly, senior managers are requiring marketers to provide compelling financial justification for their marketing plans and programs. While many view traditional marketing as an art and some view it as a science, the new marketing increasingly looks like engineering (that is, combining art and science to solve specific problems).

There will always be a central role for marketing concepts. Indeed, to make use of the powerful information tools now available requires sound conceptual grounding. But marketers need more than concepts to fully exploit the resources available to them. They need to move beyond conceptual marketing toward what we call marketing engineering: the use of interactive computer decision models to help support marketing decisions.

We designed this package of materials to supplement either a basic marketing course or a course in marketing strategy. It includes cases and exercises selected from our book, *Marketing Engineering* (Prentice Hall, 2003) that are appropriate for such courses. These selections are designed to make the corresponding material in the basic courses come alive.

Each case or exercise here is designed to accompany a specific marketing engineering software application and, if you purchased this book as a requirement for a course, the bulk of your purchase price covers an access fee for the software. You should find that software installed on your school's network.

Although each piece of software has associated with it a corresponding exercise or case problem, most of the software modules are completely independent of those cases and can be used separately on other case-problems or on real problems.

According to most marketing texts, the most common and fundamental strategic marketing problems involve segmentation, targeting, positioning and associated resource allocation decisions. We have selected and included six cases and associated software packages to correspond to that set of broad needs, as follows:

Case 1: Conglomerate's New PDA

Software: Needs-based Segmentation Using Cluster Analysis: This general software tool performs cluster analysis, factor analysis and discriminant analysis. The accompanying case addresses how to segment the market on the basis of needs for a sample of prospective buyers for a new personal digital assistant. The case raises issues such as: (1) How many segments should the firm consider (and how do those segments differ)? (2) Which of those segments should the firm target? (See GE model below). (3) How many different products should the firms offer? (also linked to GE model). (4) How should the new product be positioned? (See Positioning Analysis, below.)

Case 2: ABB Electric Segmentation

Software: Choice-based Segmentation Using Multinomial Logit Analysis: This software tool includes a multinomial logit analysis module that one can use to identify the variables that most influence customer choices, and to determine the probability that each customer will purchase each of the available choice alternatives. The accompanying case—ABB Electric—asks which of these customers or prospects are the best ones to target with a supplementary marketing program. The case introduces the concept of segmentation by switchability and shows how to use that information to profitably focus sales effort.

Case 3: Product Planning Using the GE/McKinsey Approach at Addison Wesley Longman

Software: Targeting/Business Prioritization Using GE/McKinsey Approach: This software tool allows the user to build a customized portfolio of SBUs (Strategic Business Units) and associated attribute dimensions and weights to help prioritize the businesses. The accompanying case looks at a portfolio of three new books being introduced at Addison Wesley Longman.

Case 4: Positioning the Infiniti G20

Software: Product Positioning Using Perceptual Mapping: This software tool takes customer perceptions and preferences for products and produces a two- or three-dimensional map that allows the user to view alternative product positions and consider the strategic implications of changes in that positioning. The accompanying case looks at positioning the Infiniti G20: given customer perceptions and preferences for new cars, how should Infiniti position this car in the market?

Case 5: Syntex Laboratories A

Software: Resource Allocation Using Response Models (ReAllocator): This software addresses a fundamental marketing problem: How much should I spend on marketing activity X (selling effort in this application) and how should I allocate that spending (across market segments, products, or geographic regions)? This software is applied to the Syntex Laboratories (A) Case: How large should the Syntex Labs salesforce be and how should that salesforce be deployed across products and markets? This case/software illustrates the value of market response models in resource sizing and allocation decisions even when only judgmental data are available.

Case 6: ADCAD Ad Copy Design Exercise

Software: Advertising Copy Development Using an Expert System (ADCAD): This software is a rule-based system that is designed to give advice in a qualitative decision situation. It makes specific suggestions about print advertising copy for frequently purchased products. It can be applied to a problem of the user's choosing but can also be applied (with some caution) to repositioning problems like the one faced by the Infiniti G20.

The pedagogic philosophy here involves two main principles: learning by doing and end-user modeling. What this means is that the way you will learn these concepts best is to try to apply the software to the problem and make some specific recommendations based on your experience. Thus you learn the concept by doing it yourself—not merely by studying the concept or by assigning the analysis to some staff member or consultant.

This volume contains the problem sets or cases that are keyed to each concept; you can access associated software tutorials at www.mktgeng.com. *We strongly recommend that you go through each tutorial (making sure you can reproduce the results there) before attempting to "solve" the case.* Our experience is that well over 90% of the difficulties users may encounter while running the software are solved by simply reproducing the screens in the respective tutorial. You can get other software hints (e.g., FAQ, Help files) and updates from our Web site as well, and you can also send us your comments and suggestions about the software by using the e-mail facility available at this site.

Note: if you wish to have permanent access to the software associated with this package, as well as to a number of other useful programs, you can view some options at www.mktgeng.com.

FOR THE INSTRUCTOR

Your adoption of this book for use in your course includes the delivery of a network version of the *Marketing Engineering Modules Software*. That softwear should be installed on your school's computer network by your system administrator. You and your network administrator should see www.mktgeng.com/network and follow the instructions listed there to obtain and install that software.

ACKNOWLEDGMENTS

This book grew out of the multi-year effort that we have termed Marketing Engineering and represents an evolution of our vision to put marketing modeling concepts and tools into more general use.

We gratefully acknowledge the support of the companies that sponsor Penn State's Institute for the Study of Business Markets (ISBM—the book's co-publisher), and the ISBM's Executive Director and Marketing Engineering's chief cheerleader, Ralph Oliva, for the financial and institutional support needed to make this project a continuing reality.

The preface to the first edition of the book paid tribute to the many people whose intellectual contributions and hard work made that edition possible. We redouble our thanks to all who helped make the first edition possible and we single out below those who contributed specifically to this second edition.

While we continue to write portions of the software, we are involved more in design and testing than in actual coding. Our chief software engineer, Andrew "Nuke" Stollak, together with Laurent Müllender and Daniel Soto-Zeevaert wrote most of the new code (and developed the Web site) for the second edition.

Bruce Kaplan and the staff at Prentice Hall continue to nurture this rather unusual project, helping us transform our concepts into physical reality. Ray Liddick provided exceptional production support.

Finally, we offer special thanks to Mary Wyckoff who, once again, supported and managed the whole process. She continues to put up with our unreasonable demands and unrealistic deadlines and does so with unfailing good humor.

Thanks to all!

Gary L. Lilien
•Arvind Rangaswamy
January 2002

CONGLOMERATE INC.'S NEW PDA (2001)[1]

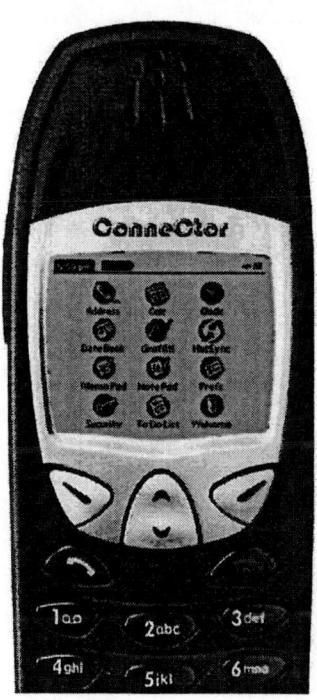

INTRODUCING THE CONNECTOR

Conglomerate Inc; a major US wireless carrier, has teamed up with a PC manufacturer to form a joint venture, Netlink, to develop, produce and market a hybrid product integrating a Personal Digital Assistant (PDA) with a "smart" cellular phone. Its first product is tentatively called ConneCtor. ConneCtor directly transmits and receives both data and voice. It is lightweight but heavier than a cell phone whose shape it emulates. It comes with a backlit grayscale LCD screen of moderate resolution. Its operating system is the PalmOS, which is common in PDAs. Thus, ConneCtor allows the user, among other things, to access the standard tools of Personal Information Management (PIM) and also performs standard cell phone functions.

ConneCtor can send and receive faxes and e-mail, access the Internet, and record voice messages. Users can input data to the PDA in the following ways:

- By typing on the on-screen keyboard
- By using the numerical keyboard
- By writing on the screen (using handwriting recognition software)
- By speaking into the phone, using a voice recorder.

---

1. This case was developed by Katrin Starke and Gary L Lilien. It describes a hypothetical situation.

An additional feature of ConneCtor is its ability to establish wireless links to other ConneCtors for voice and data transfer or to cell phones for voice transfer. For direct data transfer, the product includes an infrared port and also ships with a USB synchronization cradle. In summary, the key features of ConneCtor are:

- Instant communication for voice and data
- Cell phone, pager, fax and e-mail, and instant messaging
- PIM functions
- Digital voice recorder
- Enabled voice commands
- PalmOS application base.

THE HISTORY OF THE PDA

The Personal Digital Assistant (PDA) is basically a hand-held computer. In 1984 the first PDA, the Psion1, was introduced. It could store addresses and phone numbers, keep a calendar, and included a clock and calculator. In 1993, Apple introduced the Newton PDA, which was too bulky, too expensive, and had handwriting recognition too inaccurate to be successful. However, the excitement surrounding the Newton hinted that there could be a market for such devices. The broad acceptance of PDA technology then materialized in 1996, when Palm Inc. came out with the Palm Pilot that featured an elegant user interface and a reliable character-recognition system.

By 2001, PDAs had evolved to offer many applications including wireless Internet capabilities, games, and music playback. PDAs are designed for very specific tasks and environments: there are custom-built PDAs for amateur astronomers, truck drivers, and teachers. In addition, there is specialized software available to fit specific needs; for example, people in the medical fields can obtain software that lists thousands of drugs with their dosages and interactions.

PDA TYPES

The 2001 palm-sized PDA market was mainly composed of two types, each with its own philosophy: (1) the PDA/Palm devices run PalmOS, whose developers sought to make PDAs simple but functional products focusing on Personal Information Management (PIM) tasks; (2) the PDA/Pocket PCs run the more complex operating system, Microsoft Windows CE, which allows these PDAs to offer extensive features. In addition, "smart" phones are breaking into the PDA world. These wireless application protocol phones extend traditional cell phones with PDA functions such as email and Web access.

The original Palm Pilot embodied the PDA/Palm design mission. It provided a simple organizational device, composed of a calendar, an address book, and a to-do list with e-mail and Internet access. It also had a character-recognition system that worked for most people. Handspring, Palm's biggest competitor, introduced snap-on modules to expand the Handspring Visor and allow many applications, including an MP3 player, a web cam, and digital camera. These features appealed to the youth market and enabled Handspring to gain considerable market share. In 2001, Palm also offered this same degree of expandability and was able to maintain a market share of more than two-thirds; in addition, all of Palm's close competitors licensed its operating system, PalmOS. Several electronic manufacturers have developed similar devices; for example, Sony introduced Clie as a direct competitor to Palm and Handspring.

PocketPCs make up the other group of PDAs, whose manufacturers include Compaq, Hewlett-Packard, Psion, and Casio. These hand-held computers come with a large application suite of pocket Windows applications, e.g., a scaled-down version of MS Office. They usually come with more memory than PDA/Palms and with a range of accessories to be added to the devices (e.g., digital cameras, web cams). However, they are bulkier, heavier, and more expensive. In contrast, PDA/Palms perform basic tasks very well and, unlike the PocketPCs, synchronize with non-Windows systems.

A new technological thrust in 2001 involved the adoption of wireless technology for the PDA with manufacturers trying to assess if and how to add wireless capabilities. Wireless technology would make synchronization possible without docking, making PDAs true communication tools. AT&T, Nokia, and other cellular phone companies have started developing wireless phones with some PDA functions.

THE PDA CUSTOMER

As PDA designs have evolved, manufacturers have targeted different segments based on differing lifestyle and business needs. Palm initially captured innovators, people eager to adopt a new gadget. A typical early PDA user was a professional, high-income male. He was over 30 and probably worked in a technology field. Even as of September 2000, 93 percent of PDA users were male, according to IDC, a Massachusetts technology consulting firm.

Another major group of users is the mobile professional. Since this group frequently needs access to e-mail and the Internet while away from the office, it is also driving progress on the wireless front. A recent study by the University of California at Berkeley indicated that nearly half of the users had a technical job dealing with computers, and the overwhelming majority of the respondents rated themselves as technically sophisticated.

To attract more mainstream buyers in 2001, companies were working on increasing the usability of the PDA and its general appeal to nonbusiness users. For example, the new Claudia Schiffer Palm (sold via her Web site) is supposed to give Palm a sexier image, and Handspring's Visor line comes in many colors. Palm's affordable M series ($150) targets college students and other nonprofessional consumers. It is expected that such efforts will eventually open up the largely untapped young consumer and female market.

However in 2001, it appeared unlikely that the bulk of the mainstream population would enthusiastically embrace the PDA. A PDA was still relatively pricey and fairly limited. Handwriting recognition was slow and lacked quality, and keyboard facilities were either non-existent, too big to carry, or too small to use. The display screen was too small for most applications other than text display. Internet connections were generally both slow and expensive. In addition, the mainstream market appeared to have little need for many of the more sophisticated features the PDAs were able to offer.

PDA FEATURES

Given all the available design options, new product entries must make trade-offs between features. Customers want easy portability, but with more functions the PDA becomes heavier and bulkier. PDA users' needs are heterogeneous. Those who are looking for a high-tech way to store contact and appointment data may be satisfied with the basic models that cost $200 or less. They also are likely to prefer to keep a PC and cell phone separately rather than having an integrated PDA system that could do both. Users who plan to use the PDA as an extension of a PC by creating and accessing documents, sending e-mail, and doing basic Web surfing, might consider a Pocket-PC in the range of $350–$600. The appendix provides more details on PDA features.

FACTS ABOUT THE PDA MARKET

In 2001, many companies participated in the PDA market, bringing in a variety of new products designed to appeal to new audiences. The market was changing and growing rapidly. PDA unit sales totaled 1.3 million in 1999 and more than doubled, totaling 3.5 million in 2000 (Source: NPD INTELECT in Business 2.0). IDC, a research and analysis company, predicts worldwide sales of hand-held computing devices will reach 60 million by 2004.

In December 2000, the top five PDA brands in the United States (Source: NPD INTELECT) were:

Rank	Brand	Unit Share
1	Palm	72.1%
2	Handspring	13.9%
3	Casio	6.0%
4	Hewlett Packard	2.3%
5	Compaq	2.0%

The prices for PDAs have been relatively stable. According to NPD INTELECT, the average price of a PDA was $324 in 2000, down from $350 the year before.

THE HVC SURVEY

Netlink's management hired a market research firm, Happy Valley Consultants (HVC), to collect information about the needs of ConneCtor's potential customers. Netlink wants to use the data that HVC collected to identify segments within the market for PDAs, target appropriate segment(s) for ConneCtor, and position ConneCtor in the chosen segments.

For the targeting task, Netlink recognized that it had to develop criteria for segment selection. Using the items in Exhibit 3.6 as a starting point, Netlink identified two sets of key targeting criteria:

- Product-target market fit, in terms of Conglomerate's technical strengths, market needs and the ability of the current (or future) ConneCtors to meet those needs.
- Segment size and growth expectations, including both first purchases and upgrade/replacement buys.

THE QUESTIONNAIRE

HVC surveyed the market, looking at a range of occupation types. The survey included screening items that asked respondents if they had or would consider a PDA and if their job included time away from the office. Only those respondents who answered affirmatively to these questions were retained for further analysis.

The questionnaire asked the respondents to provide data on two kinds of variables: segmentation-basis or needs variables and variables that could be used in discriminating between or targeting the segments.

Questions for determining segmentation-basis or needs variables

X1   Whenever new technologies emerge in my field, I am among the first to adopt them.
(1 = Strongly disagree ... 7 = Strongly agree)

X2   How often do you use a pager or an Instant Messaging service?
(1 = Never ... 7 = Very often)

X3   How often do you use a cell phone?
(1 = Never ... 7 = Very often)

X4 How often do you use personal information management tools; e.g., scheduler, contact-management tools, to-do list?
(1 = Never ... 7 = Very often)

While away from your office (including remote locations)...
X5 how often do others send you time-sensitive information?
(1 = Never ... 7 = Very often)
X6 how often do you have to send time-sensitive information?
(1 = Never ... 7 = Very often)
X7 how often do you need remote access to information?
(1 = Never ... 7 = Very often)
X8 how important is it for you to share information rapidly (e.g., synchronize information) with other people, e.g., colleagues?
(1 = Not at all important ... 7 = Very important)
X9 how important is it for you to view information on a large-sized, high-resolution display?
(1 = Not at all important ... 7 = Very important)
X10 how important is it for you to have constant access to e-mail?
(1 = Not at all important ... 7 = Very important)
X11 how important is it for you to have permanent Web access; e.g., real-time stock prices, news?
(1 = Not at all important ... 7 = Very important)
X12 how important is it for you to use multimedia features; e.g., playing of music, video, and games?
(1 = Not at all important ... 7 = Very important)
X13 How important is it for you to have a communication device that is not bulky?
(1 = Not at all important ... 7 = Very important)

How much would you be willing to pay for a palm-sized PDA with the following features: instant communication from PDA to PDA, cellular phone, instant messaging, instant file sharing, e-mail, Web access, fax, personal information management features (e.g., scheduler, calculator, address book)?
X14 a) Monthly (for all services that you use)?
(1 = Not at all important ... 7 = Very important)
X15 b) Invoice price for the PDA device with all the features?
(1 = Not at all important ... 7 = Very important)

Questions for determining variables for discriminant analysis
Z1 Age
Z2 Education (1 = High school, 2 = Some college, 3 = College graduate, 4 = Graduate degree)
Z3 Income

Type of industry or occupation: (0 = No, 1 = Yes)
Z4 Construction
Z5 Emergency (fire, police, ambulance, etc.)
Z6 Sales (insurance, pharmacy, etc.)
Z7 Maintenance and service
Z8 Professional (e.g., executive, lawyers, consultants)
Z9 Computer (e.g., computer programmer, software engineer)

Z10 Do you own a PDA? (0 = No, 1 = Yes)
Z11 Do you own a cell phone? (0 = No, 1 = Yes)
Z12 Do you own or have personal access to a desktop/notebook computer? (0 = No, 1 = Yes)
Z13 How often do you spend time away from the office? (1 = Rarely ... 7 = Almost every day)

Media consumption (Readership of magazines) (0 = No, 1 = Yes)
Z14 Business week
Z15 PC Magazine
Z16 Field & Stream
Z17 Modern Gourmet

EXERCISES

1. Run cluster analysis (without Discrimination) on the data to try to identify the number of distinct segments present in this market. Consider both the distances separating the segments and the characteristics of the resulting segments.
2. Identify and profile (name) the clusters that you select. Given the attributes of ConneCtor, which cluster would you target for your marketing campaign? (Consider using a form of the GE matrix approach for this task.)
3. Rerun the analysis in Exercise 1 with Discrimination. How would you go about targeting the segments you picked in question 2?
4. How has this analysis helped you to segment the market for ConneCtor?
5. What concerns do you have with the approach (data collection, analysis, etc.) so far?
6. What are the next steps you would recommend for Netlink and the development of ConneCtor?

APPENDIX: PDA FEATURES GUIDE[2]

Operating system

There are a number of different operating systems (OS's) used for PDAs. The two main OS are PalmOS and Windows CE from Microsoft. Both license their systems to other manufacturers. Another system, EPOC from Symbian, is especially prevalent in Europe. Some manufacturers, such as Apple (Newton), use proprietary operating systems. A PDA should be compatible with the user's desktop computer. When using a PDA in a corporate environment, it is important to have compatibility with other PDAs; that way, co-workers using the same OS can swap data more easily.

Windows CE is basically a mini version of Windows, similar in look and feel to Windows 95/98. PocketPCs typically run Windows CE that Microsoft released for small devices like PDAs and set-top TV controllers. PocketPCs can only directly synch with other MS operating systems; i.e., this poses a problem for Mac users.

Palm OS is most common with palm-sized PDAs none of which come with a built-in keyboard. Developed by 3Com/Palm Computing, this is the OS for all Palm models, certain IBM Workpad models, and the Handspring Visor. The Palm OS is simple, speedy, and easily customizable via third party software and shareware programs. Its Palm OS is compatible with Windows, Mac, OS/2, Unix and Linux given the right software.

EPOC is an OS developed by Symbian, a joint venture of Psion, Ericsson, Motorola, Nokia and Matsushita. This OS is used for mobile wireless devices like smart phones as well as PDAs. In many ways, this OS resembles Windows and is fully Windows compatible. However, EPOC tends to run faster and use less power than Windows CE. With the proper software, EPOC also supports Mac, Psion, Ericsson and some others.

Screen

Most PDAs are monochrome models, but color is becoming popular. Color is more expensive, it drains batteries faster, and a color screen might wash out in direct sunlight. It is also advisable to get a screen with a backlight, which makes it easier to read under a variety of lighting conditions including the dark.

The greater a screen's resolution is, the sharper the image will be. Resolution on PDAs is limited by the compactness of the screens. On Palm units, screens are roughly 4 inches across the diagonal with resolutions up to 240 x 320.

Memory

PDAs need memory to store the operating system, standard applications, additional software, data, etc. Although more memory is usually better, storage capacity between models with different operating systems should not be directly compared, e.g., a PalmOS running model with 4 MB of RAM will store more data than a 4 MB model running Windows CE. To allow more applications to run, the memory of many PDAs can be upgraded. Other PDAs support removable storage like CompactFlash. However, greater memory leads to shorter battery life.

---

2. Source *www.viewz.com*

Ergonomics
PDAs come in a wide range of sizes: from credit card to book size. Size, weight, and hands-on feel directly influence the PDA's portability.

Synchronization
Synchronization refers to the two-way process that exchanges and updates information between the PDA and the user's computer. The connection can be via cable or, significantly slower, via the Infrared port. Most devices come with a special stand or cradle that facilitates synchronization and often recharges the PDA's batteries.

With the right software and appropriate connection, a PDA can sync with a PC remotely; for example, PDAs can access and synchronize with data stored on a corporate network. Other programs allow syncing over the Internet by keeping the information on a web server. When using the same OS, users swap information by syncing their PDAs with another user's devices, e.g., using Infrared transfer.

Batteries
Most PDAs come with rechargeable batteries, and many also work with regular alkaline batteries. Among the rechargeable batteries, Lithium-ion–based ones are the most expensive, but they hold onto their charge longer when not in use. Battery life also depends on how extensively the PDA is used. Monitoring the life of the battery is useful to avoid losing all data in case of power failure.

Modem and online services
Mobile access to the office/home PC is possible with a PDA modem or cable adaptor. Most PDAs support at least optional modems. For complete mobility, a wireless modem and wireless network access are needed.

Web
Monitor size and quality constraints strain the Web-surfing experience. However, there are several special Web browsers for PDAs that reformat regular Web content so it can be viewed on a PDA. "Web clipping" services exist that answer requests by sending back stripped down "clips" of information from participating sites. Other applications, like ProxiWeb, use proxy servers to reformat Web content before it gets sent. Lastly, PDAs can be used to download web content for offline viewing—even if the PDA does not have a modem; every time the user synchronizes the PDA, the Web content is updated through the user's PC Internet connection.

E-mail, etc.
A PDA can be used to read, write, send, and receive e-mail either by synchronizing e-mail with a desktop or directly online by using a modem. The writing of e-mails, however, is cumbersome on most PDAs, especially if there is no keyboard. Applications also exist for Usenet, and instant messaging.

Handwriting recognition
PalmOS-based devices and PocketPCs come with a touch-screen and handwriting recognition software for writing text. PDA/Palm handwriting recognition programs require that the user learn a predefined set of pen strokes to form characters. Some handwriting pro-

grams let the user customize standard pen strokes to suit the user's writing style. For Windows CE, there is a full recognition application (no pen strokes to learn) available that allows writing anywhere on the screen, but recognition is slower and uses more memory.

Other software
A PDA comes bundled with a variety of software: e.g., synchronization software, PIM applications (calendar, addresses, to-do-list, etc.), and handwriting recognition software. In addition, there is plenty of third-party commercial software, shareware, and freeware available —at least for PalmOS, Windows CE, and EPOC, but not for PDAs with a proprietary OS.

Accessories
Sync cradles or cables are usually included in the price of the PDA. Internal modems are sometimes included in the upfront price, but add-on or wireless modems are extra. Other accessories include small keyboards for palm units, AC adapters, and styluses that double as pens and bar scanners. Protective screen overlays or carrying cases are also available to increase durability and style.

Audio
PDAs have differing audio capabilities. Virtually all have built-in speakers for alert noises. Others have internal microphones for recording notes or limited voice recognition uses. Depending on the device, there may be jacks for headphones or external microphones. Audio features will be especially important for users who want to use a PDA for multimedia purposes, e.g., watching video clips or listening to MP3s. In general, PocketPC units offer more audio features, although there are add-on audio accessories for Palm OS devices as well.

ABB ELECTRIC SEGMENTATION CASE[1]

HISTORY

In March 1970, ABB Electric was incorporated as a Wisconsin-chartered corporation with initial capital provided by ASEA-ABB Sweden and RTE Corporation. The new firm's management was to operate independently of the parent company. The company mission was to design and manufacture a line of medium-sized power transformers to market in North America. The firm produced such electrical equipment as transformers, breakers, switchgears, and relays used in distributing and transmitting electrical energy. Four main types of customers buy this electrical equipment: (1) investor-owner electrical utilities (IOUs), the largest segment; (2) rural electrification cooperatives (RECs); (3) municipalities; and (4) industrial firms. Most of ABB Electric's customers were electrical utilities.

SITUATION IN 1974

After three years of operation, ABB Electric was approaching the breakeven point when it encountered a serious problem. Its market share in 1974 was around 6 percent. In 1974, total industry sales of electrical equipment dropped 50 percent compared to 1973. Further ABB Electric was a small player in an industry dominated by large competitors such as General Electric, Westinghouse, and McGraw-Edison.

ABB Electric faced several other issues at this time. The salesforce relied on traditional methods of selling and was not well focused. The salespeople acted independently and did whatever they thought they needed to do to close sales quickly. At the same time, the board of directors was pushing for standardization of products and cost reduction. The board felt that to compete effectively against the larger companies and to improve its current position of marginal profitability, ABB Electric would need a cost advantage. The directors thought this particularly important because all the major competitors made good-quality products that were similar to ABB Electric's. ABB Electric would have to find some way to differentiate itself in the marketplace.

Virtually all of ABB Electric's sales were to one type of customer, the investor-owned electrical utilities. Because these utilities already had substantial inventories, sales to this group were projected to fall as much as 80 percent per year for the next two or three years. ABB's salesforce focused most of its effort on this market segment. As a result the company had little penetration among the over 3,000 RECs and over 100,000 small municipalities and industrial companies who tended to purchase occasionally or only once. Westinghouse, General Electric, and McGraw-Edison were well-established, long-time suppliers to RECs, municipalities, and industrial customers.

NEW STRATEGY AT ABB ELECTRIC

ABB Electric's research indicated that the market for electrical equipment would remain flat well into the 1980s. This would cause downward pressure on the prices of all products sold to customers in this market. Daniel Elwing, president and CEO of ABB Electric, concluded that the only way ABB Electric could grow in this environment would be to in-

---

1. Case developed by Katrin Starke and Arvind Rangaswamy. It describes a real situation using hypothetical data.

crease its market share. This meant that ABB Electric had to steal customers away from its competitors.

To support its new marketing strategy, ABB Electric decided to develop a marketing information system (MKIS) to support decision making. To seed the MKIS database, ABB Electric hired a marketing research firm to conduct a survey to provide information about customer needs. This firm thought that it was critical that ABB Electric understand the diverse problems and needs of its potential customers better than its competitors. It also felt that such information would be useful for segmenting the electrical equipment market and would contribute toward making ABB Electric a customer-driven company. ABB Electric hired Professor Dennis H. Gensch to develop segmentation models and to show its employees the value of using formal models to implement its segmentation strategies.

ESTABLISHING THE MKIS PROGRAM

ABB Electric hired a marketing research company to design a survey to determine the product attributes most important to current and potential customers. A pretest questionnaire asked electrical equipment purchasers to rate the importance of 21 product and service attributes (e.g., maintenance requirements, invoice price, and warranty) and then to rate the major suppliers in the industry on a poor to good scale on each attribute.

The firm used factor analysis techniques (see Chapter 3 of the text) to analyze the responses to determine nine important and fairly independent attributes that influence the purchase of electrical equipment. It mailed its final questionnaire to 7,000 key decision makers at utilities, RECs, municipalities, and industrial firms who purchase electrical equipment. Respondents evaluated each supplier known to them on the nine selected attributes. They also gave an overall rating to each supplier and indicated the supplier from whom they had purchased a particular type of equipment the last time they purchased it.

Sample Survey Question

Supplier Performance Rating
List the suppliers you are considering or would consider when purchasing your next substation:

_____   _____
_____   _____
_____   _____

For each supplier on your list, indicate your perception of this supplier on the following attributes:

Invoice Price	Poor	Good
Supplier A	|————————————|
Supplier B	|————————————|
Supplier C	|————————————|
Supplier D	|————————————|

The firm received completed questionnaires from 40 percent of the sample. In a follow-up phone check of nonrespondents, it detected no significant nonresponse bias. This data formed the nucleus of the MKIS database.

Data analyses indicated that the following attributes were the most important to customers when deciding to purchase electrical equipment (not in order of importance):

- Invoice price
- Energy losses
- Overall product quality
- Availability of spare parts
- Problem-solving skills of salespeople
- Maintenance requirements
- Ease of installation
- Warranty

Professor Gensch held the view that different segments of customers would weight these attributes very differently in selecting suppliers, partly because they differed in technical sophistication and partly because they were subject to different sales-force call patterns and different promotional efforts. After reviewing the data, the marketing staff decided on three ways to distinguish between companies: by type, size, and geographic location.

CHOICE MODELING

In addition to determining the important attributes as stated by customers, Professor Gensch suggested that ABB Electric determine the most important factors based on the supplier choices customers actually made. He thought that what customers say is important may not match what actually is important when they decide on suppliers. To get at this, he developed a choice model based on multinomial logit analysis. He then developed a segmentation scheme based on the probability that a customer would choose a particular supplier (the probabilities sum to 1 for each customer):

ABB Electric Loyal Segment (Loyal): Customers in this segment have a probability of purchasing from ABB Electric that is *significantly higher* than the probability that they would buy from the next closest competitor.

Competitive Segment (Competitive): Customers in this segment have a *slightly higher* probability of purchasing from ABB Electric than from the next most preferred supplier. Thus the probability of purchasing from ABB Electric is highest, but not significantly above the probabilities of purchasing from one or more competitors.

Switchable Segment (Switchable): Customers in this segment have a *slightly lower* probability of purchasing from ABB Electric than their most preferred supplier. Thus the probability of purchasing from a competitor is highest, but not significantly higher than the probability of purchasing from ABB Electric.

Competitor Loyal Segment (Lost): Customers in this segment have a *significantly lower* probability of purchasing from ABB Electric than from their most preferred supplier. Thus these customers are highly likely to buy only from a competitor and can be classified as lost customers.

ABB Electric used this segmentation scheme to focus its sales effort primarily at the Competitive and Switchable segments. It redesigned its entire marketing program with this in mind. The salesforce spent more time calling on prospects in these segments. ABB customized its brochures to focus on the "hot buttons" specific to each segment. Most important it continuously updated the MKIS database with new data and it institutionalized this approach to targeting across the organization.

POSTSCRIPT: SITUATION IN 1988

ABB Electric has strengthened its position well beyond expectations. Its market share reached 40 percent in 1988. Along with a larger market share came improvements to its profitability. The overall market remains flat and forecasters predict that it will remain flat into the near future. However, ABB Electric was able to establish a competitive edge against much larger competitors.

EXERCISES

Suppose you are the regional sales manager for ABB Electric, and you have been given a budget for a supplementary direct marketing campaign aimed at 20 percent of the companies in your region.

1. At present you have information about the location of customers (districts 1, 2, and 3) and the sales potential of each account or prospect. Based on this information alone, to what companies would you direct the new direct marketing program? Specify the accounts and customer or prospect types.
2. Use the choice modeling approach based on the responses provided by 88 firms from your region. The data consists of the evaluation of ABB Electric and the three main competitors on eight variables: (1) Price, (2) Energy losses, (3) Maintenance requirements, (4) Warranty, (5) Availability of spare parts, (6) Ease of installation, (7) Salesperson problem solving support, and (8) Perceived product quality. Perform a customer-loyalty–based segmentation for your customers and prospects.

    - Which variables are the key drivers of choice in this market?
    - Based on your analyses, on which firms would you focus your efforts?

3. Assume that marketing efforts targeted at companies in the Loyal and Lost categories result in no incremental gain. On the other hand, suppose that you could retain or win half the companies in the Switchable and Competitive segments with this program. How much improvement in sales productivity can you realize by applying this choice model to the allocation of your efforts?
4. What other recommendations would you offer to ABB Electric to improve its segmentation marketing program?
5. Comment on the uses and limitations of this modeling approach.

PRODUCT PLANNING USING THE GE/MCKINSEY APPROACH AT ADDISON WESLEY LONGMAN CASE[1]

It was July 1997 and Mark Roth, manager of business books at Addison Wesley Longman, was facing a bit of a dilemma. He was about to present his 1998 fiscal year new book budget and had three new marketing books in his portfolio. One of them, *Marketing Engineering*, was a bit different from the other two. It did not currently have a large natural market but might ultimately be a big winner, he thought, if it were promoted properly. He was about to make his plans for annual promotion, kicking his program off at the August American Marketing Association Educator's Conference in Chicago. His main question was—How should he prioritize the promotional resources for the three new books?

BACKGROUND

Addison Wesley Longman is one of the largest global educational publishers, selling books, multimedia and learning programs in all major academic disciplines to the primary, secondary, higher education, professional, and English language teaching markets throughout the world.

AWL is part of the Pearson Group. Pearson PLC, headquartered in London, is an international provider of media content and is composed of information, education and entertainment companies. Pearson reported the following fiscal year-end figures:

1996 Sales ($ mil.): $3,746.8
1-Yr. Sales Growth: 19.5%

1996 Net Inc. ($ mil.): $413.1
1-Yr. Net Inc. Growth: (7.7%)

1996 Employees: 17,383
1-Yr. Employee Growth: (10.5%)

In addition to AWL, some of Pearson's companies include: the Financial Times Newspaper, Penguin/Putnam, The Economist Group, Pearson Professional, and Pearson Television. In 1988, Addison-Wesley was acquired by Pearson PLC. The Company merged with Longman, a sister Pearson publisher, in 1995 and became Addison Wesley Longman. In 1996, AWL acquired HarperCollins Educational Publishers, consisting of HarperCollins College and Scott Foresman, and merged those operations with AWL's.

Each company that makes up AWL has historic publishing strengths and accomplishments. Many people in the United States remember learning to read with Elson Basic Readers featuring Dick, Jane and Spot. Scott Foresman, their publisher, celebrated its centennial in 1996. Longman, which published Dr. Samuel Johnson and Wordsworth, among other British literary lights, has a distinguished 273-year tradition. The former HarperCollins College, now part of the Higher Education Publishing Group, traces its roots back to 1817 when the

---

1. Note: The individuals, events and details in this case are fictional and were created purely for pedagogic purposes. The background about AWL and the three books is real, however.

brothers Harper established a publishing house in New York City. When Melbourne Wesley Cummings published MIT physics professor Francis Sears's Mechanics in 1942, Addison-Wesley was launched as an outstanding publisher of science, mathematics and computer texts.

The college division of AWL markets books to colleges and universities throughout the world. Its main promotional resources are sampling, brochures, direct mail, exhibitions (primarily at academic meetings) and direct selling to professors. The US college division salesforce includes over 200 individuals, each of whom specializes in an academic specialty (business, science, humanities) and works in a regional territory, servicing several dozen schools. AWL managers believe that their salesforce is particularly important in encouraging instructors to consider and adopt new textbooks, and they use their salesforce as a key tool in their product introduction mix.

The new marketing texts
The three new marketing texts that AWL was introducing in the summer of 1997 were:

Advertising and Sales Promotion Strategy by Gerard J. Tellis, USC, aimed primarily at MBA advertising and sales promotion courses;

Analysis for Strategic Marketing by Vithala R. Rao, Cornell University and Joel H. Steckel, New York University, aimed at capstone MBA strategic marketing courses, particularly those with analytic content; and

Marketing Engineering by Gary L. Lilien and Arvind Rangaswamy, Penn State, a book and extensive package of software to deliver marketing tools to support marketing decision making.

The *Marketing Engineering* book was a bit different from others in that it included two volumes plus a CD with 26 software packages that could be applied immediately to both classroom and prototype professional business problems. However, as the book was sufficiently different from anything else on the market, both Mark and the authors felt that the AWL selling effort could make a critical difference in the acceptance of the book, especially in the short run.

The new marketing book promotional challenge
As Mark was finalizing his proposal, he began glancing through the *Marketing Engineering* book. He noticed that the book identified several methods that could be used to approach a problem just like his.

"What a novel idea," he thought. "Why not use the ideas and tools from *Marketing Engineering* to determine what to do here?"

He determined that one *Marketing Engineering* tool might be appropriate for his problem: the GE/McKinsey approach.

Applying the GE approach
Mark found the GE approach implemented in *Marketing Engineering* in a tool called Portfolio Planning (GE). In consultation with his planning staff, Mark came up with the following factors for the components of the composite dimensions:

Chapter 3: Product Planning Using the GE/McKinsey Approach

Industry Attractiveness:
- Market size (total volume of books to be sold in the next three years).
- Growth rate (annual growth rate of market size).
- Technological requirements[2] (high would be "traditional book," low would be when the book needed capabilities of producing multimedia, software, etc.).
- Leading edge[2] (low would include more traditional topics; high would include new and emerging topics).

Business Strength:
- Market share (book's likely share of market after two to three years).
- Share growth (annual growth rate of market share).
- Investment/cost[2] (high means low need for investment; low means high need for investment).
- Synergy (ability of book to induce sales of other AWL books or to lead to signings of new authors).

Mark then attempted to assign weights (from 1 to 5) to the factors above. He decided that the weights depended on the strategic position of the firm—whether it wanted to view itself as a traditional publisher or as a leading-edge publisher. Hence he constructed two sets of weights: "Traditional," and "Leading Edge" (Exhibit 1). He also rated each of the businesses, Tellis, Rao/Steckel, and L&R on each of the factors (Exhibit 2).

	Traditional Weights	Leading-Edge Weights
Industry Attractiveness		
Market size	5	2
Growth rate	2	5
Technological requirements	5	1
Leading edge	1	5
Business Strength		
Market share	3	2
Share growth	1	5
Investment/cost	5	1
Synergy	1	5

EXHIBIT 1
AWL's weights for new marketing texts (1-5 scale)

---

2. Note: Because of the way the GE approach works, "high" means better for the firm, "low" means worse. So, "high cost" gets a low rating and "low cost" gets a high rating.

	Tellis	Rao/Steckel	Lilien/Rangaswamy
Sales Potential	20	15	12
Industry Attractiveness			
Market size	5	3	2
Growth rate	2	4	4
Technological requirements	4	5	1
Leading edge	2	3	5
Business Strength			
Market share	3	2	2
Share growth	3	4	4
Investment/cost	4	5	1
Synergy	1	3	5

EXERCISE

Mark was planning to allocate his new product budget equally across the books. Using the GE approach:

1. Describe the business portfolio and the options available to AWL.
2. What does the GE approach suggest about the relationship between AWL's strategic objectives and its promotional plans?
3. What should Mark do?
4. What other factors should Mark consider in setting and allocating the budget?
5. Comment on the uses and limitations of the GE model.

Appendix: Details of the Three Books from AWL Promotional Material

1. *Advertising and Sales Promotion Strategy*

First Edition, 475 pages, 1998, Cloth, 0-321-01411-1

Gerard J. Tellis, University of Southern California

Unique; theoretically rigorous, rich with examples, and useful for designing successful strategies.

Promotion is a rich topic that integrates perspectives from a number of disciplines including marketing, economics, psychology, anthropology, and operations research. It is also a dynamic area that is constantly changing as firms develop new media, appeals, and methods to better compete with their rivals in a rapidly changing environment. *Advertising and Promotional Strategy* is designed to communicate all of these aspects of promotion. After reading this book, prospective managers will understand the topic of promotion well enough to be able to design successful strategies.

Hallmark Features

- Tellis's writing is simple, direct, and lively. He uses short sentences and simple language even when explaining complex ideas.
- The text has a managerial orientation—more so than any other text in the field—helping prospective managers understand the topic well enough to design successful strategies.
- The book's presentation is practical, analyzing a large number of relevant examples and describing creative promotional strategies.
- Tellis draws from the most recent research in the social sciences to ensure that students are exposed to the most current knowledge in the field.
- This book explains why phenomena occur and tries to show why certain strategies succeed, while others fail.
- Using contemporary examples, the author clearly communicates points.
- Tellis explains theories, concepts and terms from first principles—his book requires no particular prerequisites in business, marketing, economics, or psychology.
- Special topics include coverage of regulation (Chapter 2), direct marketing (Chapter 16), ethics, international strategy, and brand equity.
- Your students will enjoy the text's 16-page color advertisement insert, lavish examples and numerous illustrations.

Supplements include: Instructor's Manual with Test Bank/Transparency Masters/CD-ROM Guide, a Computerized Test Bank for Windows, a Videotape with advertisement clips for classroom use, an Instructor's CD-ROM with ad stills and clips, and an Interactive CD-ROM case on Intel that allows the student to act as a marketing manager designing a promotional strategy.

This title has the following supplements:

Instructor's Resource Manual by Siva K. Balasubramanian, Southern Illinois University includes the Instructor's Manual, Test Bank, Transparency Masters, and CD-ROM Guide. 0-321-40771-7

Instructor's CD-ROM includes a gallery of print advertisements and quick-time clips of TV commercials. 0-321-01643-2

Videotape contains advertisement clips for classroom use. 0-321-40772-5

Intel Case CD-ROM for Windows by John Quelch, Harvard University Business School, is based on a Harvard Case Study on the Advertising Campaign for Intel on introducing its product into the UK market. The student acts as a marketing manager with an advertising budget, who needs to decide who to target: the novice home computer buyer, the average business person who uses a computer, or the corporate purchasing manager. With this, they then develop an advertising and promotion campaign using a series of provided advertisements, etc. 0-321-02175-4

2. *Analysis for Strategic Marketing*

First Edition, 400 pages, 1998, Paper, 0-321-00198-2

Vithala R. Rao, Cornell University
Joel H. Steckel, New York University

Provides more modern scientific marketing methods for strategic marketing courses than any other book on the market.

Analysis for Strategic Marketing is the first book in the market to tie the aspects of strategic marketing and marketing research together. In fact, this book has no direct competitors—it simply fits in a class of its own. Rao and Steckel offer you this paperback book as a versatile tool to be used as a main text or supplement in your Senior undergraduate or MBA-level advanced Marketing Research or Strategic Marketing courses.

Hallmark Features
- This text contains a mid- to high-level mix of strategy and marketing research.
- Adding analysis and research tools to traditional marketing book material, *Analysis for Strategic Marketing* is considered unique.
- Offering four cases with solutions included in the Instructor's Manual, Rao and Steckel allow and encourage flexible use of their textbook.

This title has the following supplements:

Instructor's Manual Package by Marjorie Doyen, Cornell University, includes the Instructor's Manual, Test Bank, and Data Disk. 0-321-01900-8

3. *Marketing Engineering: Computer-Assisted Marketing Analysis and Planning*

First Edition, 350 pages, 1998, Cloth, 0-321-01417-0

Gary L. Lilien, Penn State and Arvind Rangaswamy, Penn State

This book integrates concepts, analytic marketing techniques, and operational software to train the new generation of marketers, helping them to become marketing engineers.

This textbook and the related course are aimed at educating and training marketing engineers to translate concepts into context-specific operational approaches using analytical, quantitative, and computer modeling techniques. As an underlying philosophy, this book links theory to practice and practice to theory. The entire textbook package is made up of three components: the main text; a CD-ROM that includes over 25 software packages as well as customized on-line help files; and a user manual that contains software tutorials, problem sets, and cases that enable the student to apply the concepts and software, providing them with an immediate learning experience. Lilien and Rangaswamy designed this primarily as a text for a one-semester, capstone MBA course, but the material has been used successfully in executive programs and in undergraduate classes as well.

Hallmark Features
- This book is so cutting-edge—integrating concepts, analytic marketing techniques, and operational software—that it has no direct competition.
- The text material provides a detailed, but user-oriented view of the marketing engineering approach to marketing problems in the information age.
- Chapter summaries highlight key points in each chapter while problem sets and cases enable students to apply the concepts and software.
- This book is uniquely packaged as three components: Text, User Manual, and CD-ROM. The 26 software packages on the CD-ROM allow students to implement the concepts in the course and to apply those concepts immediately—each package includes a customized set of online help files. The User Manual includes problem sets and cases, as well as a tutorial for each software package with step-by-step instructions.
- The videotape, available to adopters, provides award-winning examples of how concepts and tools have been applied profitably in a number of companies, saving them millions or even billions of dollars.

Created by the authors out of Penn State University, the book's Web site can be used for problems and continuing software updates and upgrades, so that adopters can continue to upgrade the software as it evolves.

This title has the following supplements:

> Videotape that provides award-winning examples of how concepts and tools have been applied profitably in a number of companies, saving them millions or even billions of dollars. 0-321-00775-1

> Instructor's Manual/Solutions Manual/Transparency Masters/Instructor's CD-ROM with PP. The Instructor's CD-ROM contains a complete PowerPoint Presentation for the professor to illustrate key concepts in each chapter. 0-321-03042-7

POSITIONING THE INFINITI G20 CASE[1]

INTRODUCING THE G20

In April 1990, Nissan's Infiniti division planned to introduce the G20 in the United States, adding a third model to the existing Infiniti line. The G20 was already available in Europe and Japan under the name Primera. The car, equipped with a four-cylinder engine developing 140 horsepower, would be Infiniti's entry-level luxury car. Initial market response to the G20 in the United States was disappointing, and management wondered how it might retarget or reposition the car to improve its market performance.

BACKGROUND

In 1989, three years after Honda first introduced its Acura line, Toyota and Nissan attacked the U.S. luxury car market, a segment previously dominated by American and German manufacturers.

In November 1989, Nissan launched its new luxury Infiniti division with the $40,000 Q45 as its lead car and the $20,000 M30. However, Nissan was somewhat late: in August 1989, three months before Nissan shipped its first Infiniti, Toyota had introduced Lexus, its luxury brand, with a two-car line comprising the $40,000 LS400 and the entry-level LS250.

As the figures for January to September 1990 showed, Lexus outsold Infiniti by 50,000 to 15,000. The reasons for Infiniti's slow start were threefold:

- First, the Infiniti Q45 came to the market after the Lexus LS400 had established a good market position.
- Second, Lexus had two very good cars, whereas Infiniti's M30 coupe received poor evaluations from the automobile press and from customers.
- Finally, the eccentric Infiniti advertising campaign that showed scenes of nature, but not the car itself, shared some of the blame. ("Infiniti may not be doing so well, but, hey, at least sales of rocks and trees are skyrocketing," commented comedian Jay Leno.)

RESEARCH DATA

Exhibits 1–4 summarize some of the data that Infiniti had in early 1990. Data in Exhibits 1 and 2 are based on a survey of customers from its target segments, described as people between 25 and 35 with annual household incomes between $50,000 and $100,000 (when the survey was administered, the Lexus LS250 was not yet well known to the respondents to be included in the study). The three subsegments in Exhibit 1 (denoted S1, S2, and S3) are based on information provided by Infiniti managers. Exhibit 3 is derived from sales brochures describing the characteristics of each car. Exhibit 4 summarizes demographic and psychographic information about the three subsegments and was compiled from databases supplied by Claritas, Inc.

---

1. This case was developed by Katrin Starke and Arvind Rangaswamy and describes a real situation using hypothetical data.

	G20	Ford T-bird	Audi 90	Toyota Supra	Eagle Talon	Honda Prelude	Saab 900	Pontiac Firebird	BMW 318i	Mercury Capri
Attractive	5.6	4.0	4.6	5.6	4.0	5.2	5.3	3.9	5.7	3.9
Quiet	6.3	3.6	5.2	4.2	3.5	5.4	4.8	2.8	5.0	3.3
Unreliable	2.9	4.2	3.7	2.0	4.3	3.2	3.7	3.9	2.3	4.0
Poorly Built	1.6	4.2	2.6	2.1	4.3	2.8	2.8	4.4	1.8	4.3
Interesting	3.6	5.0	4.0	4.3	3.9	3.4	3.4	5.4	3.3	3.9
Sporty	4.1	4.9	3.8	6.2	4.9	5.1	4.3	5.7	4.1	5.2
Uncomfortable	2.4	4.0	2.4	3.7	4.0	3.3	2.8	4.3	3.5	4.4
Roomy	5.6	3.9	5.3	3.5	3.6	3.9	5.1	3.3	4.3	3.6
Easy to Service	4.6	4.9	3.5	4.9	4.6	5.0	3.8	4.7	4.1	4.6
High Prestige	5.4	3.5	5.6	5.3	2.8	4.7	5.7	3.8	6.4	3.3
Common	3.5	3.6	3.4	2.9	4.3	3.9	1.9	4.3	2.8	3.9
Economical	3.6	3.7	3.6	3.2	4.9	5.0	4.3	3.1	4.3	4.6
Successful	5.3	4.2	5.0	5.5	3.7	5.6	5.3	4.4	5.9	3.9
Avant-garde	4.3	3.6	3.6	4.9	4.4	3.9	4.7	4.1	3.7	4.5
Poor Value	3.4	4.3	4.3	3.5	3.6	2.6	2.9	4.3	3.3	3.8
Preferences										
Overall	6.3	3.9	6.0	5.5	4.0	6.5	6.8	3.0	6.7	4.0
Segment I (S1)	4.3	2.1	6.0	6.1	3.3	6.0	7.5	1.2	8.3	1.7
Segment II (S2)	5.9	6.0	7.7	3.5	3.1	5.5	5.4	2.5	5.4	5.8
Segment III (S3)	8.4	2.1	3.4	8.1	5.8	8.3	8.4	5.3	7.3	3.4

EXHIBIT 1
Survey results with average perception and average preference ratings on a scale from 1 to 9 (G20.DAT).

	G20	Ford T-bird	Audi 90	Toyota Supra	Eagle Talon	Honda Prelude	Saab 900	Pontiac Firebird	BMW 318i	Mercury Capri
1	4.0	7.0	8.0	3.0	4.0	5.0	5.0	1.0	4.0	5.0
2	4.0	8.0	6.0	5.0	8.0	7.0	3.0	1.0	5.0	2.0
3	8.0	5.0	9.0	4.0	1.0	7.0	7.0	2.0	4.0	4.0
4	7.0	1.0	8.0	1.0	4.0	6.0	5.0	5.0	7.0	3.0
5	8.0	8.0	8.0	3.0	5.0	4.0	3.0	2.0	8.0	6.0
6	5.0	6.0	5.0	5.0	2.0	4.0	8.0	4.0	4.0	7.0
7	3.0	9.0	7.0	4.0	4.0	3.0	6.0	4.0	3.0	6.0
8	4.0	7.0	9.0	3.0	1.0	7.0	9.0	3.0	6.0	6.0
9	8.0	6.0	6.0	4.0	5.0	5.0	1.0	2.0	8.0	7.0
10	6.0	4.0	6.0	3.0	2.0	8.0	7.0	3.0	1.0	8.0
11	8.0	6.0	8.0	4.0	6.0	8.0	7.0	1.0	2.0	7.0
12	8.0	5.0	6.0	6.0	2.0	3.0	8.0	1.0	6.0	6.0
13	4.0	2.0	9.0	4.0	1.0	5.0	5.0	4.0	8.0	5.0
14	5.0	5.0	8.0	5.0	6.0	4.0	6.0	1.0	3.0	7.0
15	6.0	5.0	9.0	1.0	3.0	6.0	8.0	3.0	6.0	3.0
16	6.0	3.0	9.0	2.0	7.0	8.0	6.0	3.0	7.0	3.0
17	8.0	5.0	8.0	1.0	1.0	8.0	9.0	2.0	5.0	4.0
18	5.0	9.0	7.0	5.0	2.0	4.0	7.0	5.0	6.0	1.0
19	6.0	7.0	9.0	6.0	2.0	6.0	3.0	5.0	4.0	5.0
20	6.0	9.0	8.0	2.0	3.0	8.0	6.0	1.0	7.0	5.0
21	7.0	7.0	9.0	4.0	1.0	3.0	4.0	1.0	4.0	3.0
22	6.0	9.0	6.0	2.0	3.0	4.0	6.0	1.0	6.0	3.0
23	5.0	4.0	8.0	4.0	1.0	4.0	1.0	1.0	8.0	5.0
24	7.0	4.0	8.0	3.0	2.0	3.0	4.0	6.0	9.0	5.0
25	4.0	9.0	7.0	3.0	1.0	7.0	2.0	1.0	5.0	7.0
26	8.0	2.0	1.0	9.0	4.0	8.0	8.0	5.0	8.0	4.0
27	8.0	6.0	5.0	8.0	4.0	8.0	7.0	7.0	5.0	1.0
28	9.0	1.0	2.0	4.0	9.0	9.0	9.0	4.0	8.0	3.0
29	9.0	2.0	4.0	8.0	7.0	8.0	9.0	8.0	5.0	6.0
30	8.0	3.0	4.0	8.0	7.0	6.0	6.0	4.0	5.0	1.0
31	8.0	3.0	2.0	9.0	5.0	8.0	9.0	5.0	7.0	5.0
32	5.0	1.0	2.0	7.0	5.0	9.0	9.0	7.0	8.0	6.0
33	9.0	1.0	4.0	9.0	6.0	9.0	9.0	5.0	9.0	2.0
34	8.0	2.0	6.0	8.0	7.0	9.0	8.0	5.0	9.0	5.0
35	9.0	1.0	7.0	9.0	5.0	7.0	6.0	6.0	4.0	1.0
36	8.0	1.0	4.0	9.0	6.0	8.0	8.0	3.0	7.0	4.0
37	9.0	2.0	3.0	9.0	5.0	8.0	9.0	7.0	9.0	6.0
38	8.0	2.0	3.0	6.0	5.0	9.0	9.0	3.0	9.0	6.0
39	9.0	2.0	4.0	9.0	7.0	8.0	7.0	7.0	9.0	1.0
40	8.0	3.0	2.0	7.0	5.0	8.0	9.0	5.0	6.0	1.0
41	9.0	3.0	4.0	8.0	8.0	9.0	6.0	2.0	9.0	6.0
42	8.0	3.0	2.0	8.0	6.0	8.0	9.0	4.0	7.0	2.0
43	9.0	2.0	1.0	8.0	6.0	7.0	9.0	5.0	9.0	5.0
44	9.0	2.0	3.0	9.0	7.0	8.0	9.0	7.0	5.0	4.0

EXHIBIT 2
Individual-level preference data, measured on a scale from 1 to 9, with higher numbers representing increased preference (G20PREF.DAT).

	G20	Ford T-bird	Audi 90	Toyota Supra	Eagle Talon	Honda Prelude	Saab 900	Pontiac Firebird	BMW 318i	Mercury Capri
45	9.0	2.0	3.0	7.0	6.0	9.0	9.0	7.0	5.0	2.0
46	8.0	1.0	2.0	9.0	5.0	8.0	9.0	4.0	9.0	4.0
47	9.0	2.0	3.0	9.0	6.0	9.0	9.0	6.0	8.0	1.0
48	9.0	3.0	6.0	8.0	2.0	8.0	9.0	4.0	8.0	4.0
49	9.0	1.0	2.0	9.0	6.0	8.0	9.0	4.0	7.0	1.0
50	9.0	3.0	6.0	9.0	6.0	9.0	8.0	8.0	7.0	5.0
51	8.0	3.0	5.0	7.0	2.0	8.0	8.0	6.0	8.0	1.0
52	9.0	5.0	4.0	7.0	1.0	2.0	5.0	1.0	9.0	3.0
53	7.0	4.0	4.0	3.0	4.0	9.0	8.0	2.0	5.0	4.0
54	7.0	2.0	6.0	5.0	3.0	7.0	6.0	4.0	8.0	6.0
55	5.0	2.0	3.0	5.0	5.0	8.0	9.0	1.0	9.0	1.0
56	4.0	5.0	6.0	5.0	4.0	9.0	8.0	4.0	6.0	4.0
57	7.0	1.0	7.0	8.0	7.0	7.0	7.0	2.0	6.0	5.0
58	5.0	3.0	3.0	7.0	2.0	8.0	7.0	2.0	9.0	6.0
59	4.0	4.0	5.0	8.0	2.0	6.0	6.0	6.0	6.0	1.0
60	8.0	4.0	9.0	4.0	5.0	5.0	5.0	2.0	7.0	4.0
61	8.0	4.0	5.0	4.0	3.0	6.0	8.0	3.0	7.0	4.0
62	7.0	5.0	7.0	7.0	6.0	6.0	6.0	5.0	7.0	3.0
63	8.0	2.0	2.0	4.0	5.0	8.0	8.0	1.0	9.0	2.0
64	5.0	6.0	4.0	7.0	4.0	4.0	5.0	1.0	8.0	1.0
65	7.0	4.0	4.0	6.0	5.0	3.0	6.0	1.0	6.0	4.0
66	8.0	2.0	9.0	3.0	5.0	7.0	8.0	4.0	6.0	2.0
67	3.0	5.0	8.0	7.0	6.0	3.0	8.0	2.0	9.0	6.0
68	6.0	1.0	3.0	5.0	2.0	9.0	7.0	2.0	6.0	5.0
69	6.0	3.0	8.0	8.0	5.0	8.0	6.0	3.0	3.0	1.0
70	7.0	2.0	8.0	8.0	3.0	9.0	7.0	4.0	4.0	5.0
71	7.0	1.0	7.0	7.0	8.0	8.0	9.0	1.0	9.0	1.0
72	6.0	5.0	5.0	5.0	4.0	6.0	9.0	4.0	8.0	2.0
73	7.0	5.0	4.0	4.0	2.0	6.0	8.0	5.0	9.0	5.0
74	8.0	5.0	6.0	6.0	6.0	7.0	7.0	4.0	8.0	4.0
75	7.0	3.0	6.0	8.0	4.0	7.0	7.0	5.0	5.0	3.0

EXHIBIT 2 cont'd
Individual-level preference data, measured on a scale from 1 to 9, with higher numbers representing increased preference (G20PREF.DAT).

	G20	Ford T-bird	Audi 90	Toyota Supra	Eagle Talon	Honda Prelude	Saab 900	Pontiac Firebird	BMW 318i	Mercury Capri
Base Price ($)	17,500	15,783	20,200	23,280	16,437	14,945	18,295	12,690	19,900	13,500
Length (Inches)	175	198.7	176	181.9	170.5	175.6	184.5	192.0	170.3	166.1
Width (Inches)	66.7	72.7	67.6	68.7	66.7	67.3	66.5	72.4	64.8	64.6
Height (Inches)	54.9	52.7	54.3	51.2	51.4	29.2	56.1	49.8	53.5	50.2
Curb Weight (lbs.)	2,535	3,600	3,170	3,535	3,100	2,740	2,825	3,485	2,600	2,487
Fuel Economy (Mpg)										
City	24	17	18	17	20	23	20	16	22	23
Highway	32	24	24	22	25	27	26	24	27	28
Horspower, SAE.net (Bhp)	140@ 6,400 rpm	210@ 4,000 rpm	164@ 6,000 rpm	232@ 5,600 rpm	195@ 6,000 rpm	135@ 6,200 rpm	140@ 6,000 rpm	240@ 4,400 rpm	134@ 6,000 rpm	132@ 6,000 rpm
Warranty, Years/Miles,	4/ 60,000	1/ 12,000	3/ 50,000	3/ 36,000	1/ 12,000	3/ 36,000	3/ 36,000	3/ 50,000	3/ 36,000	1/ 12,000

EXHIBIT 3
Some physical characteristics of the cars.

Segment Characteristics	Segment I (Western Yuppie, Single)	Segment II (Upwardly Mobile Families)	Segment III (American Dreamers)
Segment Size	(25%)	(45%)	(30%)
Education	College Grads	College Grads or Some College	College Grads or Some College
Predominant Employment	Professionals	White-Collar	White-Collar
Age Group	25–35	25–35	25–35
Predominant Ethnic Background	White	White	Mix (Asian, White)
Average Household Income	$81,000	$68,000	$59,000
Persons per Household	1.42	3.8	2.4
Percent Married	32%	75%	55%
Watch Late Night TV	27%	9%	17%
Watch Daytime TV	3%	45%	5%
Read Computer Magazines	39%	6%	10%
Read Business Magazines	58%	23%	27%
Read Entertainment Magazines	3%	14%	30%
Read Infant and Parenting Magazines	1%	17%	2%
Rent Movies	43%	85%	38%
Possess an American Express Card	48%	45%	75%
Own Investment Funds	24%	18%	47%
Go Fishing	2%	30%	3%
Sail, Scuba Dive, or Ski	49%	2%	20%

EXHIBIT 4
Data about the segments.

EXERCISES

1. Describe the two (or, if applicable, three) dimensions underlying the perceptual maps that you generated. Based on these maps, how do people in this market perceive the Infiniti G20 compared with its competitors?
2. Infiniti promoted the G20 as a Japanese car (basic version $17,500) with a German feel, basically a car that was like the BMW 318i ($20,000), but lower priced. Is this a credible claim, given the perceptions and preferences of the respondents?
3. Which attributes are most important in influencing preference for these cars in the three segments (S1, S2, and S3) shown on these maps? To which segment(s) would you market the Infiniti G20? How would you reposition the Infiniti G20 to best suit the chosen segment(s)? Briefly describe the marketing program you would use to target the chosen segment(s).
4. What ongoing research program would you recommend to Infiniti to improve its evaluation of its segmentation of the market and positioning of its G20?
5. Summarize the advantages and limitations of the software provided for this application.

SYNTEX LABORATORIES (A) CASE[1]

April 1982 found Robert Nelson, vice president of sales for Syntex Laboratories, considering the results of a salesforce size and allocation study. Those results presented Nelson with a dilemma. He had previously submitted a business plan increasing the number of sales representatives from 433 to 473. By now, the corporate budget cycle of which that plan was a part was well under way. The study, however, indicated that sales and contribution to profit for fiscal 1985 at the 473 level would be much less than could be obtained with an optimal salesforce size of over 700. Although Nelson was unsure how fast Syntex Labs could hire and train sales reps, the study clearly showed that a salesforce growth rate of only 40 reps per year would severely limit both present and future profitability.

The study results had been presented by Laurence Lewis, manager of promotion research, and Syntex Labs' liaison to the consultants that had done the analysis. Following Lewis's initial presentation, Nelson arranged a second presentation for Stephen Knight, senior vice president of marketing for human pharmaceuticals. They had agreed that the results were so dramatic that, if they had confidence in the results, they should attempt to interrupt the corporate planning cycle and request more sales reps.

COMPANY BACKGROUND

Syntex Corporation began in 1940 when Russell Marker, a steroid chemist, derived a cheap and abundant source of steroid hormones from the black, lumpy root of a vine growing wild in the jungles of the Mexican state of Veracruz. Syntex's first products were oral contraceptives and topical steroid preparations prescribed by gynecologists and dermatologists respectively. By 1982 Syntex Corporation had become an international life sciences company that developed, manufactured, and marketed a wide range of health and personal care products. Fiscal 1981 consolidated sales were $710.9 million with $98.6 million net income. Since 1971, Syntex had recorded a 23 percent compound annual growth rate.

SYNTEX LABORATORIES

Syntex Laboratories, the U.S. human pharmaceutical sales subsidiary, was the largest Syntex subsidiary. During fiscal 1981, Syntex Laboratories' sales increased 35 percent to $215,451,000, and grew as a percentage of total pharmaceutical sales to 46 percent, continuing a recent upward trend. Operating profit in 1981 was 27 percent of net sales. Syntex Laboratories developed, manufactured, and marketed anti-inflammatories used to treat several forms of arthritis; analgesics used to treat pain; oral contraceptives; respiratory products; and topical products prescribed by dermatologists for skin diseases. Syntex emphasized pharmaceutical research in support of these existing product lines, and in several important new therapeutic areas, including immunology, viral diseases, and cardiovascular medicine.

---

1. This case was prepared by Associate Professor Darral G. Clarke as the basis for class discussion rather than to illustrate either effective or ineffective handling of an administrative situation.
    Copyright ©1983 by the President and Fellows of Harvard College. No part of this publication may be reproduced, stored in a retrieval system, or transmitted in any form or by any means—electronic, mechanical, photocopying, recording, or otherwise—without the permission of Harvard Business School. Distributed by HBS Case Services, Harvard Business School, Boston, MA 02163. Printed U.S.A.

SYNTEX LABS' PRODUCT LINE

Syntex Labs' product line consisted of seven major products. Naprosyn was by far the largest and most successful, while Norinyl and the topical steroids represented Syntex's early development as a drug manufacturer. Exhibit 1 presents retail drug purchases and market shares for Syntex products.

Naprosyn

Naprosyn[2] was the third largest selling drug in the nonsteroidal anti-inflammatory (NSAIDs) therapeutic class[3] in the country, behind Clinoril and Motrin. NSAIDs were used in the treatment of arthritis.

Major selling points for Naprosyn were its dosage flexibility (250, 375, 500 mg tablets), twice-daily regimen (less frequent than for competing products), and low incidence of side effects within a wide dosage range. The NSAI market in fiscal 1980 was $478 million. Exhibit 2 has details of NSAI market trends.

The extremely competitive arthritis drug market would soon become even more competitive as other pharmaceutical firms entered the huge and fast-growing market for alternatives to aspirin in treating arthritis. According to one expert, Naprosyn would "weather the storm (of increased competition) better than any existing agent, although its share will be lower in 1985 than today."

Anaprox

Anaprox was launched in the United States early in fiscal 1981. It was initially marketed for analgesic use and for the treatment of menstrual pain. Nearly twice as many prescriptions were written for analgesics as for anti-arthritics in the United States, making this an important, but highly competitive, market. Exhibit 2 presents details on analgesic market trends.

At the end of fiscal 1981, the U.S. Food and Drug Administration approved Anaprox for the treatment of mild to moderate, acute or chronic, musculoskeletal and soft-tissue inflammation.

Topical steroids

Lidex and Synalar were Syntex's topical steroid creams for treating skin inflammations. Fiscal 1981 sales of dermatological products, Syntex's second largest product category, were only slightly ahead of sales in 1980. U.S. patents on two of the active ingredients in Lidex and Synalar expired during 1981, but other Lidex ingredients continued to be protected under formulation patents. Syntex anticipated some continued growth from these two important products and new dermatological products were under development.

During fiscal 1980, Syntex was the only established company to increase total prescription volume in topical steroids, while two new entrants grew from smaller shares. Market shares of new prescriptions and total prescriptions are shown in Exhibit 3. Syntex had a very strong following among dermatologists—21 percent of all new topical steroid prescriptions written by dermatologists were for Syntex products. Topicort, a competitor's brand, had enjoyed 65 percent growth ($3.66 million to $6.02 million) as a result of successful selling to both dermatologists and general practitioners.

---

2. All Syntex Labs product names are registered trademarks.
3. Drugs used for similar purposes were combined for reporting purposes into groups called *therapeutic classes*.

Norinyl

Total drugstore sales for oral contraceptives (OC) in 1980 were up 23 percent over the previous year, but this dollar-volume growth was primarily the result of a price increase. Total cycle[4] sales declined by 3.5 percent. New prescriptions overall declined 1.5 percent, while new prescriptions for low-dose oral contraceptives increased by 21 percent.

Syntex's oral contraceptive, Norinyl, was available in three dosages that together totaled $37 million, or 10 percent of the market. The low-dose segment was the growth segment of the OC market; 30 percent of all new prescriptions were for low-dose products. Mid-dose products accounted for 54 percent of all new prescriptions, and high-dose products, only 16 percent.

The oral contraceptive market was extremely competitive, with seven major competitors and dozens of products. Syntex's fiscal 1981 sales increase was due primarily to larger sales to the Agency for International Development than in the previous year, price increases, and the introduction of low-dose Norinyl, which was approved by the FDA in that year. Exhibit 3 contains OC market trends.

Nasalide

Nasalide was a steroid nasal spray for the treatment of hay fever and perennial allergies. It was approved for U.S. marketing early in fiscal 1982.

THE SALES REPRESENTATIVE

The sales rep's job was to visit physicians and encourage them to prescribe Syntex drugs for their patients. This was usually done by providing the physician with samples and with information about the appropriate dosage for various medical uses. Performance of this task was complicated by the difficulty of getting appointments with busy physicians, obtaining and maintaining credibility as a reliable source of information on drug use, the number of competing sales reps vying for the physician's time, and the difficulty in measuring the results of the detailing effort.

Robert Nelson described the physician visit as follows:

> A good sales rep will have a pretty good idea of what the physician's prescribing habits are. For example, most physicians are aware of Naprosyn by now, so our sales rep would try to find out what the physician's usage level is. If the physician was not prescribing Naprosyn, the sales rep would present clinical studies comparing Naprosyn with other drugs, probably stressing Naprosyn's lower incidence of side effects and its twice-a-day regimen and then request the physician to prescribe Naprosyn for their next six rheumatism patients. The same sort of information might be used to persuade a physician to move Naprosyn up from third choice to second or first choice. Physicians already prescribing Naprosyn could be encouraged to increase the dose for severe cases from 750 to 1,000 mg per day, using recent research showing Naprosyn to be safe at those levels. New uses cleared by the FDA could also be explained, or the rep might just reinforce the physician's choice of Naprosyn and counteract competitors' claims for their drugs.

The choice of which physicians to visit, how often to visit them, and what to present was a major consideration for the individual sales rep. Though sales management might set

---

4. Oral contraceptive sales were recorded by the amount of the drug used for one menstrual cycle.

quotas and provide guidelines, on a day-to-day basis the final choice was largely the rep's. Laurence Lewis explained:

> Sales reps tend to divide the physicians in their territories into two groups: "prescription-productive" physicians and "easy-to-call-on" physicians. Suppose a company sets a minimum daily call average of seven. The sales rep tries to visit the most productive physicians first; they are busy physicians for the most part, so the rep may have to wait a while to see them. Later in the day the sales rep gets nervous about making the seven calls so he fills in with easy-to-call-on physicians that might not be terribly productive. His bonus, however, is based on quota and annual sales increase over the previous year, So he can't be totally unconcerned about the productivity of the physicians he visits.

Nelson felt that once the decision had been made about the number of sales reps and the sales territories had been defined and assigned, the limits of his organizational authority had about been reached. Decisions he might make about which physician specialties to visit and what drugs to feature would be subject to individual reps' interpretation and preferences. It would be necessary to educate and motivate the reps to act in accordance with the sales plan. If the reps didn't agree with the plan, strict quotas and overly directive policies would be counterproductive.

SALES MANAGEMENT AT SYNTEX LABS

Robert Nelson had been promoted to vice president of sales from director of marketing research. In his new position, he reported directly to Stephen Knight, the senior vice president of marketing for Syntex Laboratories. Reporting to Nelson through Frank Poole, the national sales manager, were 6 regional, 47 district sales managers, and 433 general sales reps. Also reporting to him separately was a group of reps that specialized in hospital sales and dermatology sales.

After some consideration, Nelson decided he had a few major decisions of a relatively strategic nature to make in managing the salesforce: the size of the sales force and its geographic allocation were of obvious importance. Call frequency, allocation of sales calls across physician specialties, and product-featuring policies were also important decisions that were relatively difficult to change once implemented.

Sales Force Size

Data available in 1980 showed that Syntex's salesforce[5] was rather small compared with those of its direct competitors:

NSAI		Oral Contraceptives		Topical Steroids	
Upjohn	930	Ortho	330	Schering	615
Merck	955	Wyeth	724	Squibb	761
McNeil	457	Searle	405	Lederle	600
Pfizer	663			Hoechst	379

---

5. This case deals only with the general salesforce and does not include the hospital salesforce. For simplicity, "salesforce" will be used to mean the general salesforce.

It was by no means obvious to Nelson, however, how much larger the Syntex salesforce needed to be. Since each competitor had a different product line that required calling on a different mix of physician specialties. it wasn't clear how the size of the Syntex salesforce should compare with the others.

Call frequency

The 433 sales reps at Syntex had been generally adequate to support a six-week call cycle (each physician was scheduled to be visited once every six weeks) with approximately 70,000 targeted physicians. Indeed. this was how the number of reps had been determined in the first place. Since many of the physicians Syntex visited were visited by other companies with four-week call cycles, Nelson had considered that possibility.

The four-week call cycle seemed attractive for at least two reasons. First, if one believed that the sales force had a positive influence on physicians' prescribing behavior, it seemed reasonable that offering less frequent positive contact than the competition had to hurt. Second. dermatologists and rheumatologists had been visited by Syntex sales reps in nearly a four-week cycle, and these were felt to be Syntex's most successful physician specialty groups.

Allocation of sales effort across products and physician specialties

The necessity to allocate salesforce effort across various physician specialties was apparent from the number of physicians in various specialties—a total of 135,229 physicians in office-based practice. Visiting all of them in a four-week call cycle would have required at least 1,200 sales reps (assuming no geographic complications). This would have been nearly three times as large as Syntex Labs' current salesforce and nearly one-third larger than that of its largest competitor.

The Syntex sales policy called for a rep to attempt to make seven sales calls per day, during which presentations would be made for two or three Syntex products. (The average was 2.7 presentations per sales call.) Which products would be featured depended on a number of factors, such as the physician's specialty, the availability of new information on Syntex product efficacy and or comparative advantages, and national sales priorities

The fact that not all physicians were likely to prescribe all of Syntex's products complicated the choice of both product presentations and physician specialties. The fact that a sales rep could make an average of seven calls and 19 presentations in a day did not necessarily mean that a recommended product-featuring schedule could be followed exactly. For example, if the rep called on four dermatologists and three obstetricians in a particular day, there would be no opportunity to make Naprosyn presentations.

Geographic allocation of sales force

When Robert Nelson became vice president of sales, geographic allocation of the salesforce seemed to be the most critical factor, so it had received immediate attention. The problem turned out to be a reasonably tractable one, however. Gathering information about the location of physicians and competitors' sales reps was a huge data-gathering task, but as Laurence Lewis explained:

> Almost everyone deploys their sales reps based on regional physician counts. We made an effort to get away from just physician counts, and looked at market potential. I know other companies have done that. In the end, it all came down to where Lilly, Pfizer, Merck, and ourselves would all have a rep in a given geo-

graphical territory. Maybe one of the big companies would have two reps in a particular territory, but regional deployment ended up being almost standard. I don't suppose any of us have any real hope of coming up with good enough data to really override that allocation, at least at the territory level. We finally built a model at the state level which is based on six factors that are weighted differentially according to management judgment. We assumed that when we got below the state level a lot of geographical things, or whatever, would have to be taken into account. We now have a comfortable deployment scheme at the state level. But we still have to know how many sales reps we should have in total and what specialties we are going to push.

SALESFORCE STRATEGY MODEL

Nelson and Knight had observed that the rapid growth of Naprosyn was changing the balance in Syntex Laboratories. According to Knight:

We had always been a specialty-oriented company. We began with a product for dermatologists, then followed that with an oral contraceptive, so we visited OB-GYNs[6] too, and for the first 15 years those were the main physicians we visited, along with a limited number of primary-care physicians.[7] So we've thought of ourselves as a small, specialty-oriented pharmaceutical company. Along came Naprosyn and suddenly we had the ninth largest selling drug in the U.S. and we were growing at over 25 percent a year. We were being forced to rethink just what kind of a company we were. It was this dynamic change in the nature of Syntex that led us to consider a more sophisticated analysis.

According to Nelson:

We knew we had some opportunities to expand the salesforce. We could see how rapidly Naprosyn was growing and that our detailing penetration with generalist doctors was very low compared to the big anti-arthritis competitors like Upjohn and Merck. They each had 900 sales reps, so we knew we were behind them. But we were trying to make major plans on the back of envelopes! We'd make notes like: If there are 60,000 generalist doctors and we've got this many people, how many calls can we make a year if each of them makes 1,360 calls a year? How are we going to divvy up those calls? We then realized we were saying that all these doctors respond to sales reps the same way, and yet we all knew that they didn't. But we could never make the differences explicit! We were assuming all products responded the same way, and we knew that wasn't right. Finally we asked ourselves if there wasn't some better way to do this.

In an effort to find a better way, Nelson created the position of manager of promotion research. The position was filled by Laurence Lewis, an analyst in the marketing research department who had earlier been a sales rep. Lewis's first task was to identify a method for determining the size of the salesforce and allocating salesforce effort across products and physician specialties. After studying the marketing research and trade literature and con-

---

6. OB-GYN–obstetrician and gynecologist
7. Primary-care physicians (PCP) include physicians specializing in internal medicine, general practice, and family practice.

sulting other knowledgeable people, Lewis decided to approach Leonard Lodish, a professor at the Wharton School, whose name had surfaced repeatedly during his research.

Lodish was subsequently invited to visit Syntex and make a presentation on his approach to determining salesforce size and sales effort allocation. Two aspects of his approach struck responsive chords with Knight and Nelson. Nelson stated:

> One of the attractive features of the approach was getting our sales and marketing management people together and making explicit what we believed about how each of our products responds to detailing.

Knight felt that:

> Our history had been one of increasing the salesforce size in relatively small steps. I've never been really satisfied that there was any good reason why we were expanding by 30 or 50 representatives in any one year other than that was what we were able to get approved in the budget process. Over the years I'd become impatient with the process of going to the well for more people every year with no long-term view to it. I felt that if I went to upper management with a more strategic, or longer-term viewpoint, it would be a lot easier to then sell the annual increases necessary to get up to a previously established objective in salesforce size and utilization.

Subsequently, a contract was signed with Management Decision Systems (MDS), a Boston area-based management consulting firm of which Lodish was a principal, to produce a salesforce strategy model for Syntex. Laurence Lewis was appointed liaison with MDS.

Model development process

The salesforce strategy model (SSM) was designed to help Syntex management deploy the salesforce strategically. The model would be used to calculate the amount of sales effort to direct to various Syntex products and physician specialties, and to maximize the net contribution for a given salesforce size. Repeated applications of the model with different numbers of reps could be used to make decisions on the best totals.

The technique used in the model combined management science techniques with historical data and management judgment to calculate the incremental gain in net contribution for each additional amount of sales resource (either product presentations or physician calls).

Defining the model inputs

The SSM used information from various sources. The average number of presentations per sales call, the number of sales calls per day, the contribution margin for Syntex products, and the cost per sales representative were estimated from company records and syndicated data sources. (See Exhibit 4.) The current allocation of salesforce effort was a key element in developing the model, since these data provided the background for Syntex managers to use in estimating the response of various Syntex products and physician groups to different levels of sales effort.

There were two separate, but similar, versions of the SSM model. One sought to allocate the number of *sales rep visits to physician specialties* to maximize contribution, while the other sought the optimal allocation of *sales presentations to Syntex products*. Each estimated the optimal sales force size independently of the other.

The judgmental estimates of response to sales effort were obtained during a series of special meetings held in conjunction with the annual marketing planning meetings. Leonard Lodish, Stephen Knight, Robert Nelson, Laurence Lewis, Frank Poole, and a few product managers and regional sales managers participated. According to Lewis:

> The meeting began with a short lecture on sales response and an exercise in which we were each asked to come up with an optimal sales plan for a sales rep who had six accounts and four products. Trying to do this led us to understand what the model would try to accomplish and demonstrated the impossibility of trying to plan by hand for more than 400 sales reps selling six or more products to 13 different physician specialties.

The main agenda of the meetings was to come to a group consensus on the likely response of each Syntex product and physician specialty to sales rep effort. On Monday, the first day of the annual meetings, worksheets were distributed to the participants on which they were asked to estimate the change in sales for each of seven Syntex Labs' products and nine physician specialties that would result from different levels of sales rep activity. Each manager responded to the following question for each product and specialty:

According to the strategic plan, if the current level of salesforce effort is maintained from 1982 to 1985, sales of Naprosyn (Anaprox, etc.) could be the planned level. What would happen to Naprosyn's (Anaprox, etc.) 1985 sales (compared with present levels) if during this same time period it received:

1. no sales effort?
2. one-half the current effort?
3. 50 percent greater sales effort?
4. a saturation level of sales effort?

After a summary of the participants' answers had been presented to the group and discussed, new worksheets were passed out and the process repeated. When a reasonable consensus had been obtained, the meeting was recessed.

Following this meeting, a preliminary version of the model was produced. When the group reconvened on Friday, a preliminary analysis was presented and the results were discussed. The initial analysis appeared generally reasonable to the participants and, after a final discussion and some later fine-tuning, resulted in the response estimates that appear in Exhibit 5. Commenting on the process, Knight explained:

> Of course, we knew that the responses we estimated were unlikely to be the "true responses" in some absolute knowledge sense, but we got the most knowledgeable people in the company together in what seemed to me to be a very thorough discussion and the estimates represented the best we could do at the time. We respect the model results, but we'll utilize them with cautious skepticism.

According to Poole, "We did the best we could to estimate the model. At first we were uncomfortable at having to be so specific about things we weren't too sure about. but by the end of the discussions, we were satisfied that this was the best we could do."

Model structure

The salesforce strategy model assisted a manager in determining the size of the salesforce and the allocation of sales effort across products or customers by:

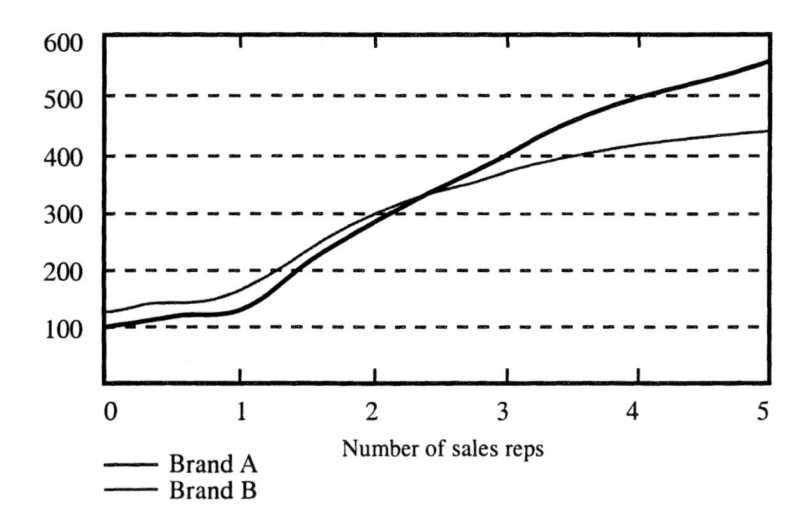

```
600
500
400
300
200
100
   0    1    2    3    4    5
              Number of sales reps
── Brand A
── Brand B
```

1. Predicting the net contribution and sales volume that would result from a particular salesforce size and allocation policy; and
2. Providing an efficient means of searching over various sales force sizes to find both the optimal sales force size and the optimal allocation policy

The basic concept of the model was quite simple: each additional sales rep should be assigned to visit the specialty which. considering the allocation of the current salesforce, would provide the highest incremental contribution. Consider the following example of a company that has

1. Two products—A and B
2. Three sales reps who sell only A, and two sales reps who sell only B
3. The response of A and B to sales effort specified below

Suppose now that the company wants to add two sales reps. The model considers the additional reps sequentially. If the first new rep is assigned to sell product A, the result will be $100 incremental contribution ($500–400). If the first new rep is assigned to sell B, only $75 incremental contribution ($375–300) will result. Thus, the first sales rep should be assigned to sell product A. The company now has 4 "A sales reps," and 2 "B sales reps." If the second new rep is assigned to sell product B, he or she could still generate $75 incremental contribution. But if assigned to sell A, only $50 could be generated.[8] So the second new sales rep should be assigned to sell B.

Exhibit 6 presents a portion of the model output allocating sales representatives to specialties. At each step in the analysis, the model indicated the number of reps already allocated, the number of new reps allocated, and to which specialty. If successive additional reps were to be allocated to the same specialty, they were accumulated in a single step.

The SSM could be used to determine the optimal number of sales reps by increasing the size of the salesforce and observing the net contribution to profit and incremental contribution per sales rep added. At each salesforce size, the salesforce was optimally deployed, and the optimal salesforce size was the one with maximum net contribution and incremental net contribution per added rep equal to zero.

---

8. The simplified algorithm presented here does not assure an optimal solution for S-shaped response curves. The actual SSM algorithm is the same in spirit as this example but has a refinement to assure an optimal solution for all reasonable response functions.

Syntex management had estimated response functions for both products and specialties, so running the model in both modes would provide a validity check on the approach in general. The specialty-based analysis indicated an optimum salesforce size of 768, and the product-based analysis 708 sales reps.

Results of the SSM analysis

The recommended optimal salesforce sizes computed on the basis of physician specialty and products were reasonably close together. The models differed considerably, however, in their estimation of incremental net contribution per added sales rep at levels between the current salesforce size and 600 reps. (See Exhibit.7.)

Not only did both SSM analyses indicate that the current Syntex salesforce was too small, it also showed that allocation was suboptimal. According to the specialty-based analysis, FY 1985 net contribution at the present salesforce size would be more than $7.2 million less than could be obtained with an optimal deployment policy. (See Exhibit 8.)

A direct comparison of present and optimal deployment according to the product-based analysis was somewhat more difficult, since the SSM indicated that Anaprox should either receive no sales attention or the equivalent of the next 130 sales reps. Nothing in between was optimal. This resulted in reported optimal salesforce sizes of 369 and 499 sales reps, but no report on the current size of 433. The SSM results were clear, however, that the current Syntex allocation of effort across products was even more suboptimal than it had been across specialists. Exhibit 9 shows that when 369 sales reps were optimally deployed across products, sales and net contribution would be $50.5 million and $45.7 million higher, respectively.

Finally, with both optimal salesforce size and optimal deployment, FY 1985 sales and contribution (see Exhibit 10) would be dramatically larger than with the current salesforce size and optimal deployment:

SSM Predicted FY 1985 Sales and Contribution from Optimal Deployment

According to	Sales Force Size	Sales ($MM)	Net Contribution($MM)
Specialty model			
(current)	434	$373.1	$221.1
	429	380.1	227.6
	768	447.7	251.7
Product Model			
(current)	430	$373.1	$222.2
	369	423.6	264.2
	708	485.9	279.6

Management implications

Robert Nelson had expected that the salesforce would be found to be too small and that Naprosyn probably needed more emphasis, but no one had anticipated that the optimal salesforce size would be between 700 and 800 reps. According to Laurence Lewis:

> When Len [Lodish] asked how far out he should run the thing, we were standing at 430 reps and I said. "Why don't you run it out to 550 or the maximum, whichever comes first." We knew we weren't paying enough attention to Naprosyn because our major NSAI competitors outnumbered us so far, and

that's our biggest and most important market. We also knew that Naprosyn was our most important product, but we didn't really know to what *degree* it was our most important product. We had the perception that a lot of the attention given to launching three new products had been at the expense of our smaller products, but the model showed it had come out of Naprosyn and that was exactly what we hadn't wanted to happen.

When he received the SSM analyses, Lewis decided four major conclusions could be drawn from them:

1. Until the size of the salesforce approaches 700 general representatives, profitability will not be a constraint to adding representatives.
2. From the FY 1981 base of roughly 430 representatives, Syntex Labs should grow to an optimal allocation of sales effort rather than by redeploying the current salesforce. This could be done by devoting additional sales resources largely to the primary-care audience.
3. Naprosyn was the largest product in Syntex's product line, the most sales-responsive, and highly profitable. Thus Syntex Labs should make it the driving force behind nearly all deployment and allocation decisions.
4. Syntex should consider itself a major generalist company, since optimal deployment would require the greatest portion of a large salesforce to be devoted to the generalist physician audience.

Although enthusiastic about these conclusions, Lewis added a note of caution to their acceptance:

A significant change in the marketplace that would decrease the ability of any of our products to compete would challenge the validity of the model output. Such phenomena as a product recall or a revolutionary new competitive product might act to reduce the value of this model.

Significant error in the sales response estimates of either products or specialties could lead to reduced validity of model output. The similarity between the two model outputs derived from independent response estimates hints at the low likelihood of significant error in the sales response estimates. The model would be most sensitive to significant error in the estimate of Naprosyn's sales responsiveness.

Lewis had concluded his presentations of the study results by stating that Robert Nelson and Stephen Knight were faced with two choices if they decided not to expand the salesforce to an optimal size. They could:

1. Optimize the physician sales call allocation with a smaller than optimal sales force by dramatically reducing coverage of specialists to increase calls on primary-care physicians. This option would maximize sales for the number of sales reps by leading to large gains in Naprosyn at the expense of sales losses in oral contraceptives and topical steroids.
2. Limit Naprosyn's growth to substantially less than its potential, while maintaining the present contact levels with Syntex's traditional specialist physicians and older products.

	Retail Drug Purchases (000s)			Total RX (000s)		
	July 80–July 81	81–82	%	80–81	81–82	%

Therapeutic Class

NSAI (anti-arthritics)
Market	$477,834	$533,980	+16%	49,759	51,466	+3%
Naprosyn	90,448	114,242	+26%	6,837	7,849	+19%
Syntex share	18.92%	21.42		13.7%	15.3%	

Analgesic (pain killers)
Market	$315,324	$346,784	+1%	89,774	91,881	+2%
Anaprox	8,119	13,027	+60%	762	1,569	+106%
Syntex share	2.5%	3.8%		0.8%	1.7%	

Oral Contraceptives
Market (all forms)	$359,942	$442,669	+23%	50,811	53,896	+6%
Syntex total	36,925	50,726	+37%	5,636	5,865	+4%
Syntex share	10.3%	11.42		11.1%	10.9%	

Topical Steroids (skin ointments)
Market	$138,895	148,895	+7%	24,948	24,531	+2%
Syntex products	31,361	37,768	+20%	5,181	5,241	+1%
Syntex share	22.6%	25.4%		20.8%	21.4%	

	New RX (000s)		
	80–81	81–82	%

Therapeutic Class

NSAI (anti-arthritics)
Market	23,829	24,569	+3%
Naprosyn	3,323	3,656	+10%
Syntex share	13.9%	14.9%	

Analgesic (pain killers)
Market	65,976	67,160	+2%
Anaprox	591	1,040	+76%
Syntex share	0.9%	1.5%	

Oral Contraceptives
Market (all forms)	13,730	13,182	–0.4%
Syntex total	1,620	1,520	–7%
Syntex share	11.8%	11.5%	

Topical Steroids (skin ointments)
Market	15,345	15,009	–2%
Syntex products	3,044	3,103	+2%
Syntex share	19.8%	20.7%	

EXHIBIT 1
Syntex Laboratories (A) Recent Sales Trends in Syntex*
*Compiled from IMS data

Nonsteroidal anti-inflammatory market trends

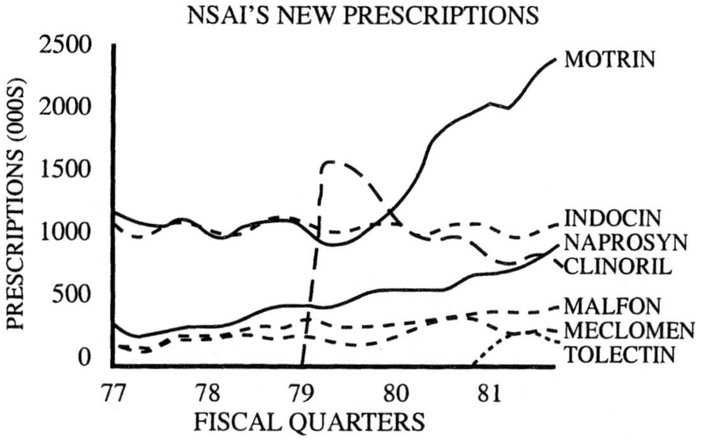
NSAI'S NEW PRESCRIPTIONS
PRESCRIPTIONS (000S)
2500
2000
1500
1000
500
0
77
78
79
80
81
FISCAL QUARTERS
MOTRIN
INDOCIN
NAPROSYN
CLINORIL
MALFON
MECLOMEN
TOLECTIN

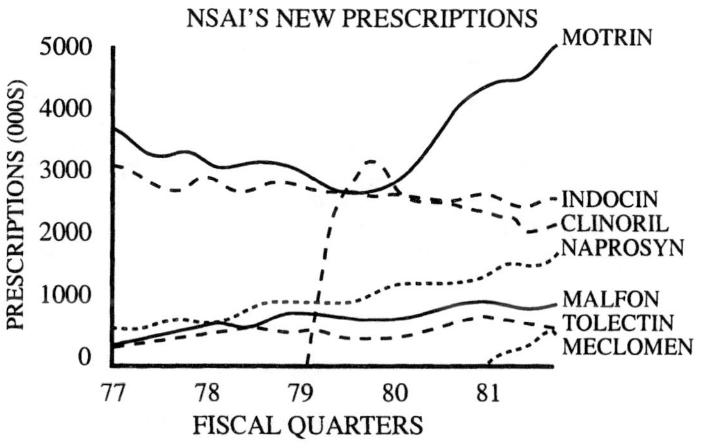
NSAI'S NEW PRESCRIPTIONS
PRESCRIPTIONS (000S)
5000
4000
3000
2000
1000
0
77
78
79
80
81
FISCAL QUARTERS
MOTRIN
INDOCIN
CLINORIL
NAPROSYN
MALFON
TOLECTIN
MECLOMEN

EXHIBIT 2
Syntex Laboratories (A)

Analgesic (drug store only) market trends

ANALGESICS NEW PRESCRIPTIONS

Y-axis: PRESCRIPTIONS (000S), 0 to 5000
X-axis: FISCAL QUARTERS, 77 to 81

Series: TYL/COD, PROPOXY, EMP/COD, DARVOCET-N, ZOMAX, DARVON/CMP, TALVIN, ANAPROX

ANALGESICS TOTAL PRESCRIPTIONS

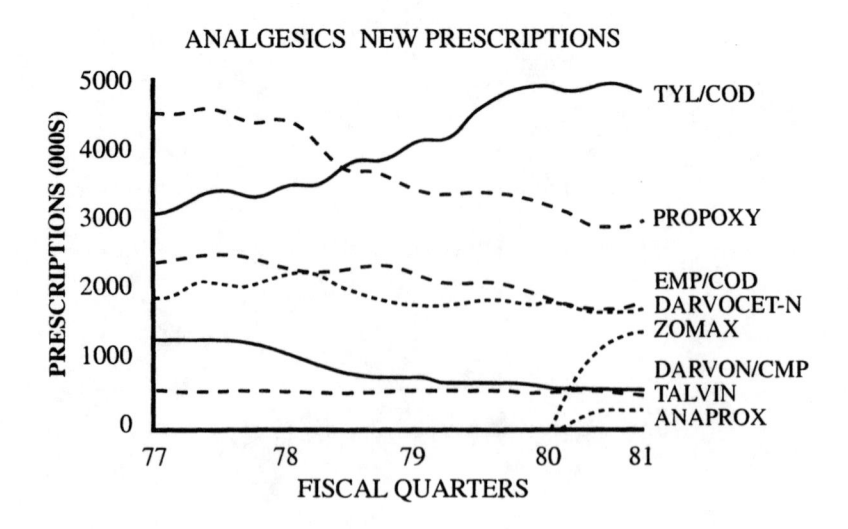

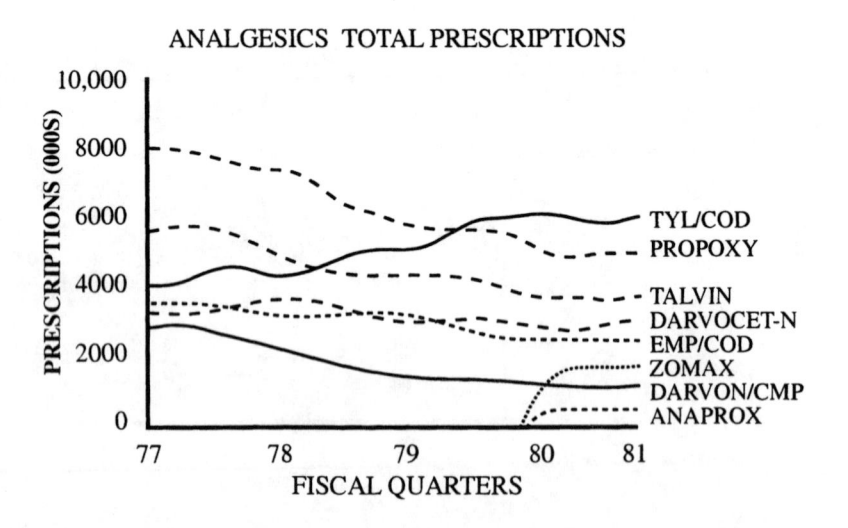

Y-axis: PRESCRIPTIONS (000S), 0 to 10,000
X-axis: FISCAL QUARTERS, 77 to 81

Series: TYL/COD, PROPOXY, TALVIN, DARVOCET-N, EMP/COD, ZOMAX, DARVON/CMP, ANAPROX

EXHIBIT 2 cont'd.
Syntex Laboratories (A)

Topical steriod market trends

TOPICALS NEW PRESCRIPTIONS

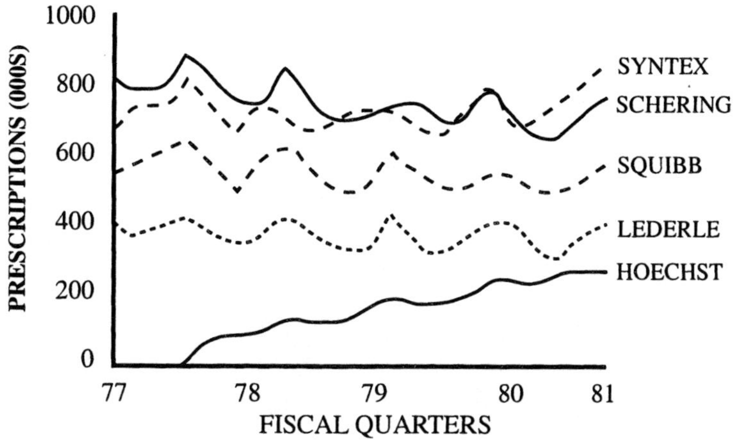
1000
800
600
400
200
0
PRESCRIPTIONS (000S)
77
78
79
80
81
FISCAL QUARTERS
SYNTEX
SCHERING
SQUIBB
LEDERLE
HOECHST

TOPICALS NEW PRESCRIPTIONS

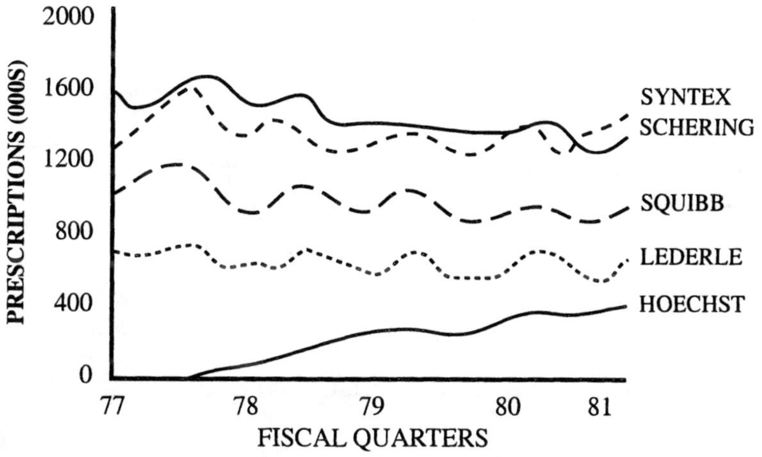
2000
1600
1200
800
400
0
PRESCRIPTIONS (000S)
77
78
79
80
81
FISCAL QUARTERS
SYNTEX
SCHERING
SQUIBB
LEDERLE
HOECHST

EXHIBIT 3
Syntex Laboratories (A): Topical steriod market trends

Oral contraceptive market trends

OC'S NEW PRESCRIPTIONS

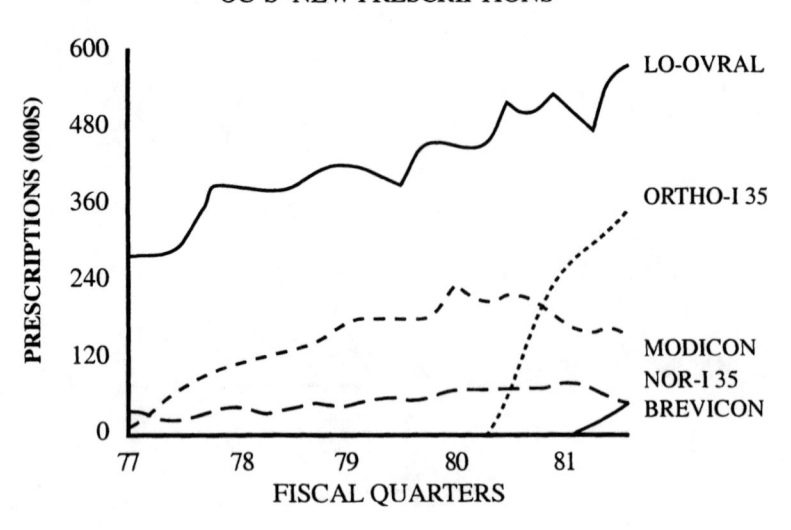

OC'S CYCLE VOLUME

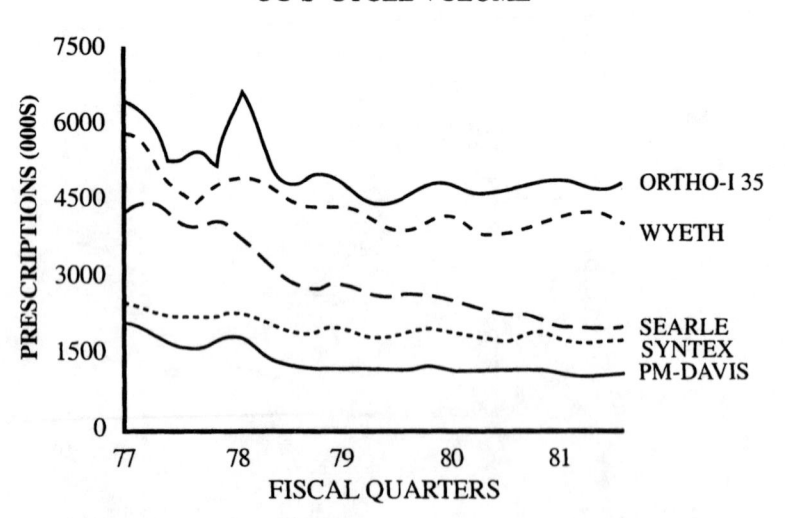

EXHIBIT 3 cont'd.
Syntex Laboratories (A): Topical steriod market trends

Normal planned 1985 calls or presentations based on FY 1981.

Products (Presentations)		Specialties (Calls)	
Naprosyn	358,000	General practice	124,000
Anaprox	527,000	Family practice	108,000
Norinyl 135	195.000	Internal medicine	98,000
Norinyl 150	89,000	Orthopedic surgeon	54,000
Lidex	101,000	Rheumatologist	13,000
Synalar	110,000	Obstetrician/	
Nasalide	210,000	gynecologist	117,000
TOTAL	1,590,000	Dermatologist	50,000
Aver/rep.	3,677	Allergist	14,000
		Ear, nose, throat	12,000
		TOTAL	590,000
		Aver/rep.	1,360

Planned 1985 sales ($000) with present policy (Syntex 1985 estimates by product, allocated to specialties on FY 1981 product by specialty distribution).

Product		Specialty	
Naprosyn	$214,400	General practice	$92,398
Anaprox	36,500	Family practice	78,083
Norinyl 135	21,200	Internal medicine	79,082
Norinyl 150	37,200	Orthopedic surgeon	19,671
Lidex	38,000	Rheumatologist	16,961
Synalar	14,600	Obstetrician/	
Nasalide	11,200	gynecologist	51,312
TOTAL	$373,100	Dermatologist	26,598
		Allergist	3,434
		Ear, nose, throat	5,561
		TOTAL	$373,100

Contribution as percent of Factory Selling Price.

Product		Specialty	
Naprosyn	70%	General practice	67.6%
Anaprox	55	Family practice	67.8
Norinyl 135	72	Internal medicine	68.1
Norinyl 150	72	Orthopedic surgeon	68.4
Lidex	62	Rheumatologist	67.5
Synalar	53	Obstetrician/	
Nasalide	52	gynecologist	66.2
		Dermatologist	55.3
		Allergist	62.5
		Ear, nose, throat	62.2

Estimated 1985 average cost per representative (excluding samples) $57,000.
Estimated 1985 fixed selling overhead (present organization) $2,800,000.

EXHIBIT 4
Syntex Corporation (A) Basic Model Inputs*
* 1985 plans have been disguised.

Product Response Functions

	No Calls	One-Half	Present	50% More	Saturation
Naprosyn	47	68	100	126	152
Anaprox	15	48	100	120	135
Norinyl 135	31	63	100	115	125
Norinyl 150	45	70	100	105	110
Lidex	56	80	100	111	120
Synalar	59	76	100	107	111
Nasalide	15	61	100	146	176

Specialty Response Functions

	No Calls	One-Half	Present	50% More	Saturation
General practice	29	62	100	120	136
Family practice	31	62	100	124	140
Internal medicine	43	69	100	111	120
Orthopedic surgeon	34	64	100	116	130
Rheumatologist	41	70	100	107	112
Obstetrician/ gynecologist	31	70	100	110	116
Dermatologist	48	75	100	107	110
Allergist	17	60	100	114	122
Ear, nose, throat	20	59	100	117	125

EXHIBIT 5
Syntex Laboratories (A)

Step No.	No. of Reps.	Chg. In Reps.	Sales (000s)	Chg In Sales (000s)	Net Profit (000s)	Chg. In Net Profit Per Rep (000s)	Alloc. To:
26	391.8	0.9	367,818	312.4	224,144	185.7	RHEU
27	392.6	0.8	368,119	300.5	224,285	176.0	ENT
28	428.7	36.1	380,052	11,933.4	230,390	169.1	ORS
29	437.0	8.3	382,766	2,713.5	231,752	164.3	GP
30	463.7	26.7	393,586	10,820.2	235,995	158.7	DERM
31	470.9	7.2	395,871	2,285.4	237,133	157.6	FP
32	477.5	6.6	397,911	2,039.6	238,149	155.0	IM
33	480.8	3.3	399,201	1,290.2	238,646	148.7	DERM
34	481.6	0.8	399,463	262.2	238,763	146.3	ENT
35	489.4	7.8	401,814	2,350.5	239,873	142.0	OBGYN
36	493.0	3.6	402,863	1,049.4	240,385	141.9	ORS
37	493.9	0.9	403,114	251.1	240,505	138.1	RHEU
38	502.2	8.3	405,412	2,297.6	241,586	130.4	GP
39	509.7	7.5	407,603	2,191.4	242,529	125.9	ALLG
40	510.6	0.9	407,874	270.8	242,645	123.9	ALLG
41	517.8	7.2	409,787	1,913.1	243,530	122.7	FP
42	524.4	6.6	411,452	1,665.1	244,291	116.1	IM
43	525.2	0.8	411,659	206.4	244,374	103.0	ENT
44	533.5	8.3	413,610	1,951.8	245,221	102.2	GP
45	534.4	0.9	413,814	203.8	245,309	101.3	RHEU

Key:
GP   general practice
FP   family practice
IM   internal medicine
ORS   orthopedic surgeon
RHEU   rheumatologist
OBGYN   obstetrician/gynecologist
DERM   dermatologist
ALLG   allergist
ENT   ear, nose, throat

EXHIBIT 6
Syntex Laboratories (A): Syntex Laboratories Sales Force Strategy Model Specialty Allocation.

Contribution to profit versus number of sales reps.

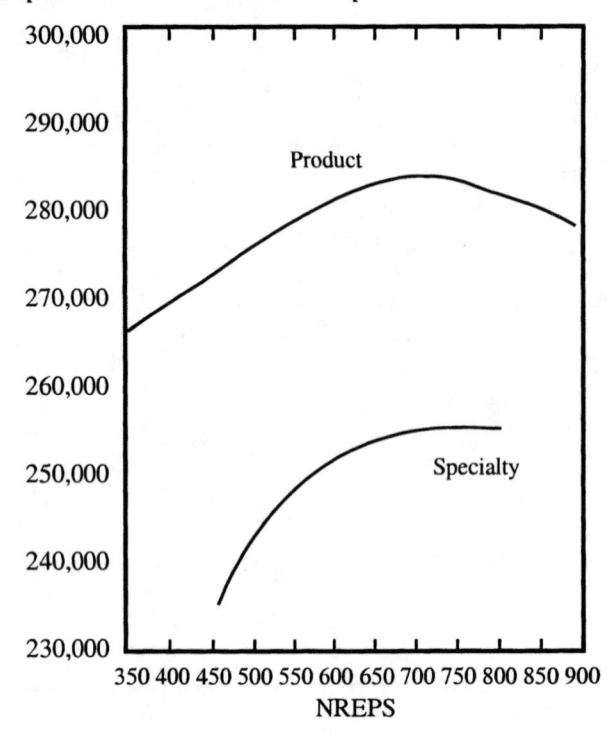

Marginal contribution versus number of sales reps.

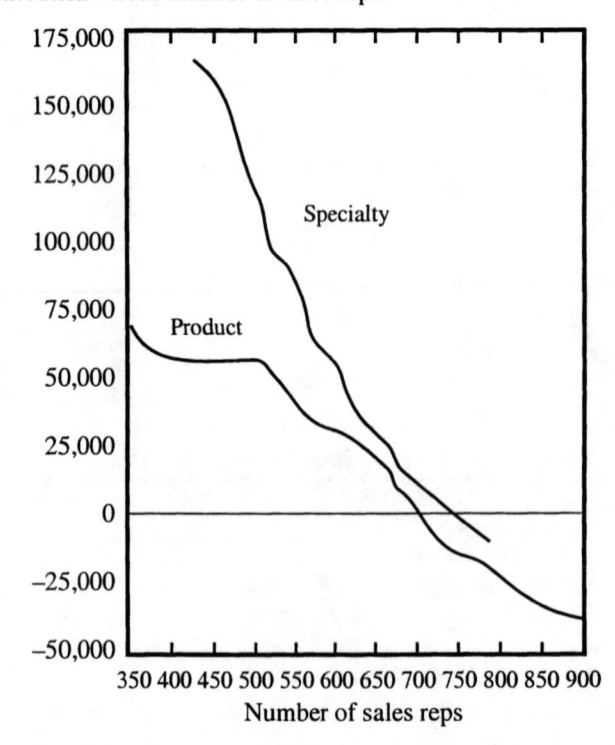

EXHIBIT 7
Syntex Laboratories (A)

Present Policy

Allocation to	Number of Reps	Sales Calls	Sales in Dollars (000s)	Gross Profit (000s)	Net Profit (000s)
GP	91.2	124,000	92,398	62,461	56,715
FP	79.4	108,000	78,083	52,940	47,938
IM	72.1	98,000	79,082	53,855	49,313
ORS	39.7	54,000	19,671	13,455	10,954
RHEU	9.6	13,000	16,961	11,449	10,844
OBGYN	86.0	117,000	51,312	33,969	28,551
DERM	36.8	50,000	26,598	14,709	12,390
ALLG	10.3	14,000	3,434	2,146	1,497
ENT	8.8	12,000	5,561	3,459	2,905
Total	433.8	590,000	373,100	242,837	221,106

SSM Recommended Policy

Allocation to	Number of Reps	Sales Calls	Sales in Dollars (000s)	Gross Profit (000s)	Net Profit (000s)
GP	116.0	157,818	103,915	70,246	63,632
FP	108.3	147,273	92,624	62,799	56,627
IM	78.6	106,909	81,586	55,560	51,079
ORS	36.1	49,091	18,622	12,737	10,680
RHEU	10.4	14,182	17,273	11,660	11,065
OBGYN	70.4	95,727	47,120	31,194	27,181
DERM	0.0	0	12,767	6,805	6,805
ALLG	0.0	0	584	365	365
ENT	8.8	12,000	5,561	3,460	2,956
Total	428.7	583,000	380,052	254,825	227,590

Key:
GP   general practice
FP   family practice
IM   internal medicine
ORS   orthopedic surgeon
RHEU   rheumatologist
OBGYN   bstetrician/gynecologist
DERM   dermatologist
ALLG   allergist
ENT   ear, nose, throat

EXHIBIT 8
Syntex Laboratories (A): Comparision of Existing Policy with Recommended Policy at Current Salesforce Levels *
(1985)
* Optimal allocations are only computed for salesforce sizes in a step (see Exhibit 6). A consequence of this is that allocations are not available for every salesforce size and thus allocated sales force sizes don't exactly match the current level.

Present Policy

Allocation to	Number of Reps	Presentations	Sales in Dollars (000s)	Gross Profits (000s)	Net Profit (000s)
N	96.8	358,000	214,400	150,080	143,981
A	142.4	527,000	36,500	20,075	11,104
N 135	52.7	195,000	21,200	15,264	11,944
N 150	24.1	89,000	37,200	26,784	25,266
L	27.3	101,000	38,000	23,560	21,840
S	29.7	110,000	14,600	7,738	5,867
N	56.8	210,000	11,200	5,824	2,246
Total	429.7	1,590,000	373,100	249,325	222,247

Recommended Policy 369 Reps

Allocation to	Number of Reps	Presentations	Sales in Dollars (000s)	Gross Profits (000s)	Net Profit (000s)
N	246.3	911,272	306,526	214,568	200,530
A	0.0	0	5,475	3,011	3,011
N 135	57.5	212,727	22,019	15,854	12,576
N 150	28.4	105,181	38,049	27,394	25,774
L	37.2	137,727	41,222	21,847	19,726
S	0.0	0	8,614	4,565	4,565
N	0.0	0	1,680	873	873
Total	369.4	1,366,909	423,585	288,115	264,257

Recommended Policy 499 Reps

Allocation to	Number of Reps	Presentations	Sales in Dollars (000s)	Gross Profits (000s)	Net Profit (000s)
N	246.3	911,273	306,527	214,569	200,530
A	129.5	479,091	33,708	18,539	11,159
N 135	57.5	212,727	22,019	15,854	12,577
N 150	28.4	105,182	38,048	27,395	25,774
L	37.2	137,727	41,222	21,848	19,726
S	0.0	0	8,614	4,565	4,565
N	0.0	0	1,680	874	874
Total	498.9	1,846,000	451,819	303,644	272,405

EXHIBIT 9
Syntex Laboratories (A): Comparision of Existing Policy with Recommended Policy at (Near) Current Levels

Optimal Sales Force Policies

Based on Specialties

Allocation to	Number of Reps	Sales Calls	Sales in Dollars (000s)	Gross Profit (000s)	Net Profit (000s)
GP	198.9	270,545	118,680	80,227	68,888
FP	173.3	235,636	104,067	70,558	60,682
IM	131.0	178.182	90,700	61,767	54,299
ORS	61.4	83,454	22,818	15,608	12,110
RHEU	16.5	22,454	18,327	12,371	11,430
OBGYN	117.3	159,545	55,389	36,667	29,980
DERM	43.4	59,091	27,551	14,685	12,208
ALLG	12.2	16,546	3,667	2,292	1,599
ENT	13.6	18,546	6,506	4,047	3,270
Total	767.6	1,044,000	447,706	298,221	251,665

Based on Products

Allocation to	Number of Reps	Sales Calls	Sales in Dollars (000s)	Gross Profit (000s)	Net Profit (000s)
NAPROSYN	263.9	976,363	309,379	216,565	201,524
ANAPROX	168.3	622,818	39,847	21,915	12,321
NORINYL 135	76.7	283,636	24,068	178,329	12,959
NORINYL 150	37.2	137,545	39,060	28,123	26,004
LIDEX	49.6	183,636	43,155	22,872	20,043
SYNALAR	29.7	110,000	14,600	7,738	6,043
NASALIDE	82.6	305.455	15,802	8,217	3,512
Total	708.0	2,619,454	485,911	322,761	279,606

Key:
GP   general practice
FP   family practice
IN   internal medicine
ORS   orthopedic surgeon
RHEU   rheumatologist
OBGYN   obstetrician/gynecologist
DERM   dermatologist
ALLG   allergist
ENT   ear, nose, throat

EXHIBIT 10
Syntex Laboratories (A)

ADCAD AD COPY DESIGN EXERCISE

1. The best way to learn to use the ADCAD system is to develop the key components of a commercial for a familiar brand, such as Pepsi or Coke. In doing so, keep a specific target segment in mind and compare the recommendations of the system with a recent brand commercial targeted to that segment.
2. Another way to use the ADCAD system is to develop ads for brands whose strategic context is described as a business case. In particular, the Suave Shampoo case (Harvard Business School cases 9-585-019 and 9-585-020) and the Johnson's Wax I case (Harvard Business School case 9-583-046) are good for this purpose.
3. Use the recommendations to develop a one-page print advertise-ment for the product you chose for analysis. Indicate from the system how you used the recommendations in developing your print ad.
4. Summarize the advantages and limitations of the ADCAD system for developing ad-copy-design parameters.
5. After using the ADCAD system, a senior ad agency executive commented, "This is precisely the type of systematic approach that I would like our creatives to use. They need to develop an appreciation of the strategic rationale for an ad before they let their creative juices flow." On the other hand, after using the system, an art director commented, "Developing an ad is like making an omelet. McDonald's will consistently make us a halfway decent omelet but it takes a great chef to make one that we will remember for long. I don't think creatives will accept a mechanistic approach to ad design."

Do you agree with either of these two points of view? Explain why or why not.